MW01617914

Kim Lim: Space, Rhythm & Light

Space, Rhythm & Light

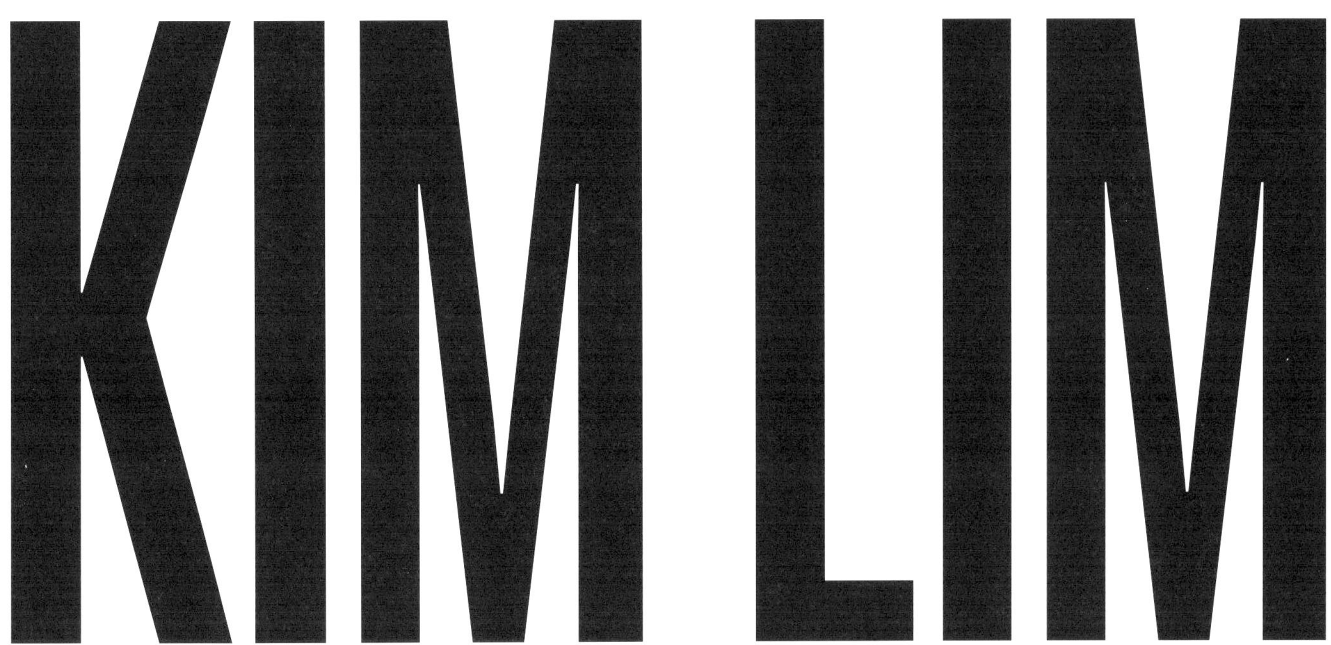

Edited by **Abi Shapiro**

with contributions by **Bianca Chu**
Joleen Loh
Hammad Nasar
Adele Tan
Wenny Teo and
Ming Tiampo

THE HEPWORTH WAKEFIELD
LUND HUMPHRIES

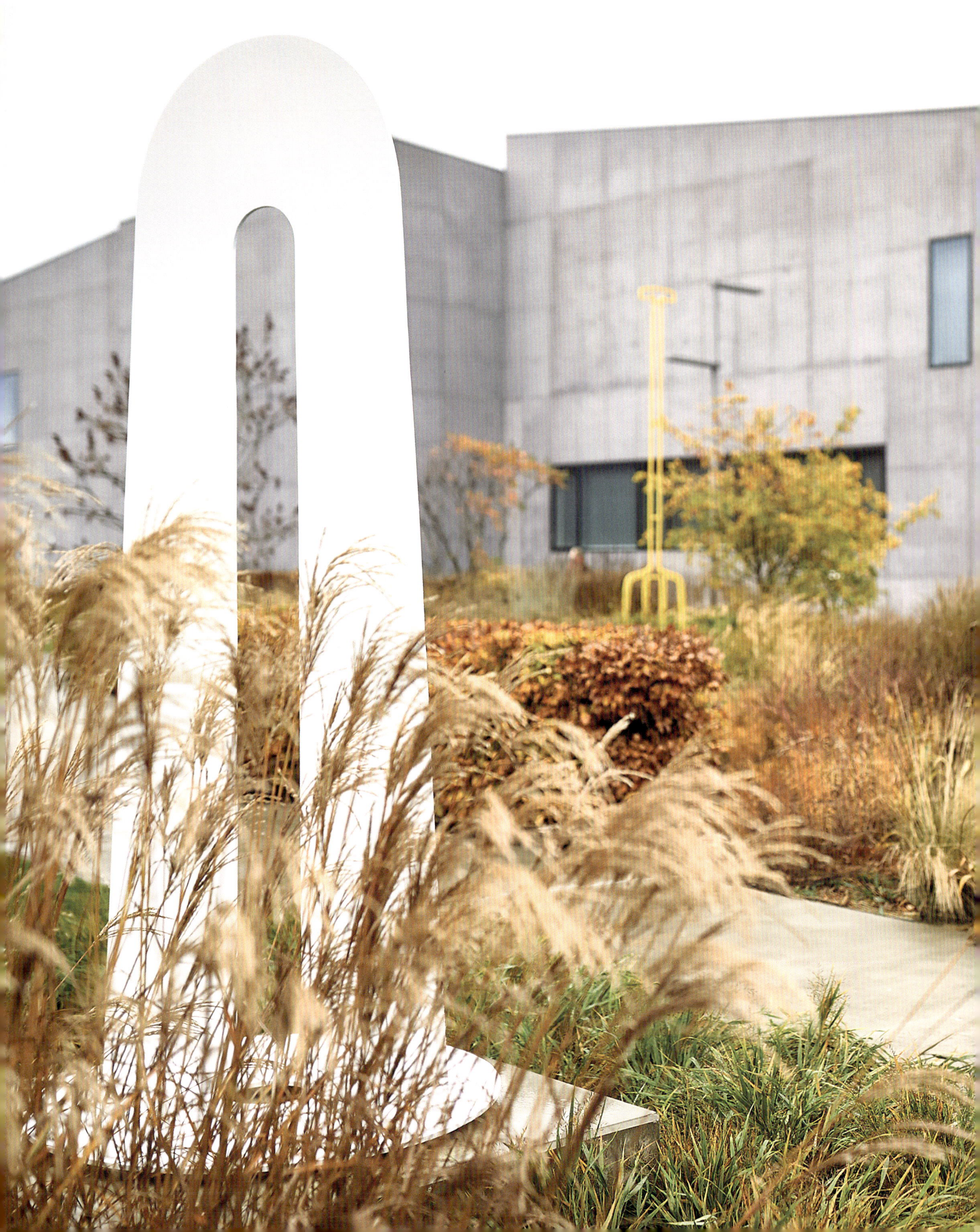

Director's Foreword

The exhibition *Kim Lim: Space, Rhythm & Light* at The Hepworth Wakefield is the first major institutional public retrospective of the artist's career in over 20 years, and we are delighted to share this long-overdue survey that revisits her work and life.

The British-Singaporean artist's history with Wakefield Art Gallery inspired the initiation of this project. *Day* (1966; fig.1) was acquired for Wakefield's collection in 1983 and put on display in the garden. The sculpture was first seen by the public in Battersea Park in London in 1966 in the exhibition *Sculpture in the Open Air*, where it was sited among sculptures by artists including Henry Moore, Anthony Caro, Elisabeth Frink and Barbara Hepworth. This was the first of many dialogues between the abstract forms of Lim and Hepworth. Today, the two artists are once again exhibited together in The Hepworth Wakefield Garden, where *Day* continues to act as a sun dial, casting its reaching shadow across the ever-changing seasonal plants and foliage.

The Hepworth Wakefield offers an ideal context in which to experience the many shared qualities and themes that link the art of Hepworth and Lim. Not only did both artists develop innovative sculpture and prints based on their experience of the natural world, but both understood the interrelated techniques of carving and printmaking whereby engagement with form, space, rhythm and light could be fruitfully translated between three and two dimensions. Re-activating dialogues between Lim and Hepworth contributes valuably to the important ongoing expansion of 20th-century British sculptural histories.

The exhibition would not have been possible without the generosity of those who lent to the exhibition including: Arts Council Collection, Southbank Centre, London; Collection of Chong Huai Seng and Ning Chong, Singapore;

1 **Day** in The Hepworth Wakefield Garden, 1966 painted steel, 215 × 96·3 × 2 cm (85 × 38 × 1 in)
Wakefield Council Permanent Art Collection (The Hepworth Wakefield).

the Estate of Kim Lim and William Turnbull; Tate; and private lenders in the UK. Special thanks go to Bianca Chu, Johnny Turnbull and Alex Turnbull at the Estate of Kim Lim who have been incredibly generous with their time, supporting all aspects of the exhibition as well as this publication. Their dedication, warmth and care have been crucial in enabling us to realise this project.

The exhibition was generously supported by an exhibition grant from the Henry Moore Foundation as well as Michael and Yvonne Uva, and the publication was supported by a publication grant from the Paul Mellon Centre for Studies in British Art. I'd like to extend my gratitude to those who produced thoughtful and important contributions to this book, including Wenny Teo, Hammad Nasar, Ming Tiampo, Adele Tan, Joleen Loh, Bianca Chu and Abi Shapiro, as well as the enthusiastic team at Lund Humphries, particularly Lucy Clark, Sarah Thorowgood, Rebeccah Williams and Michela Parkin.

We would like to thank Wakefield Council and Arts Council England for their significant investment in the gallery. It is vital to our work and success, and we are proud to provide a significant return on their investments.

Thank you, as ever, to the entire team at The Hepworth for all their superb work, with particular thanks to our Curator Abi Shapiro who conceived of the exhibition as well as edited and contributed to this publication. She was ably assisted by our Curatorial Assistant Farah Dailami, Exhibition and Collections Manager Eleanor Dobson and Gallery Manager Karl Vickers.

Simon Wallis
Director, The Hepworth Wakefield

2 Kim Lim with **Chess Piece I** (1960), *c.*1960 The Estate of Kim Lim

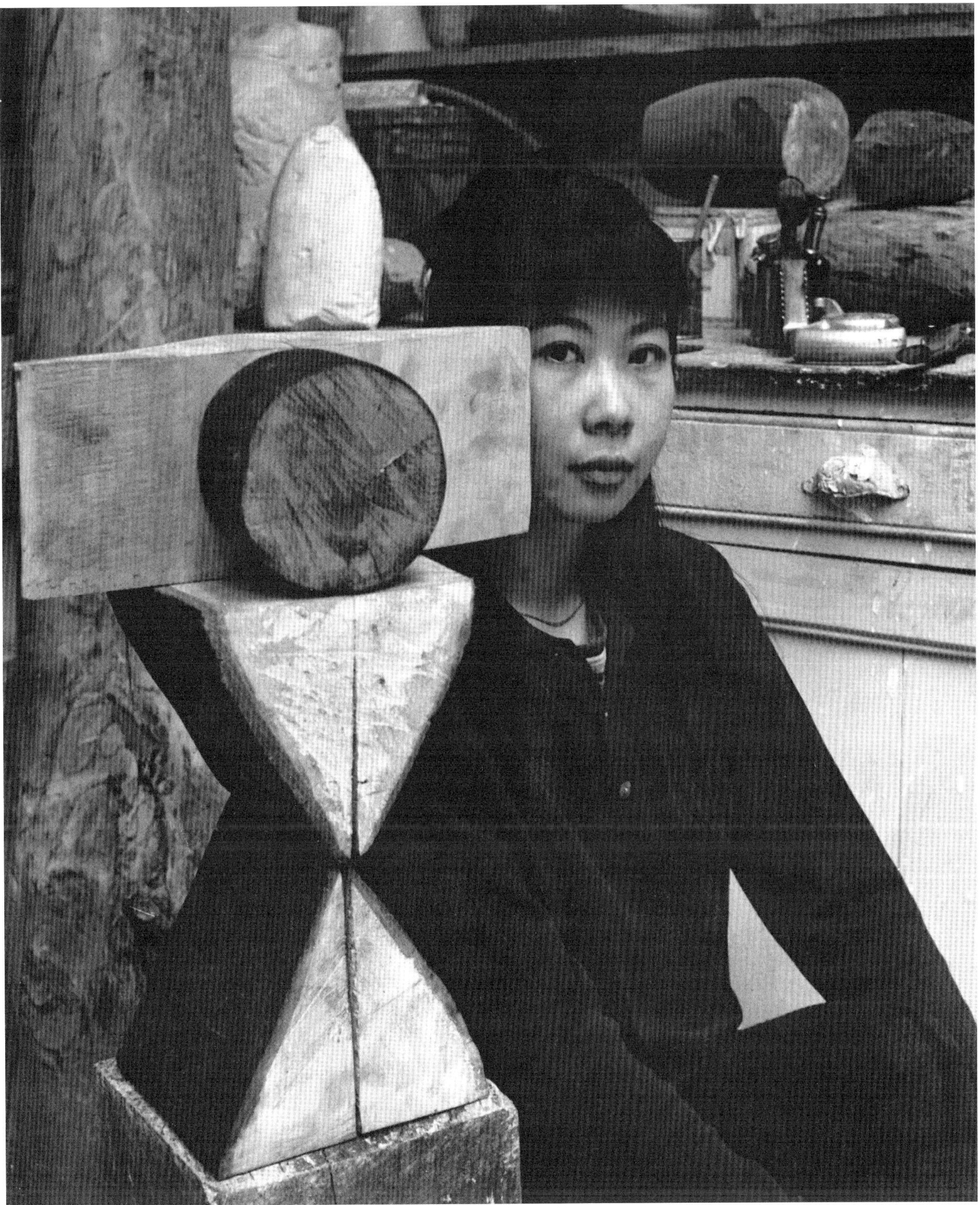

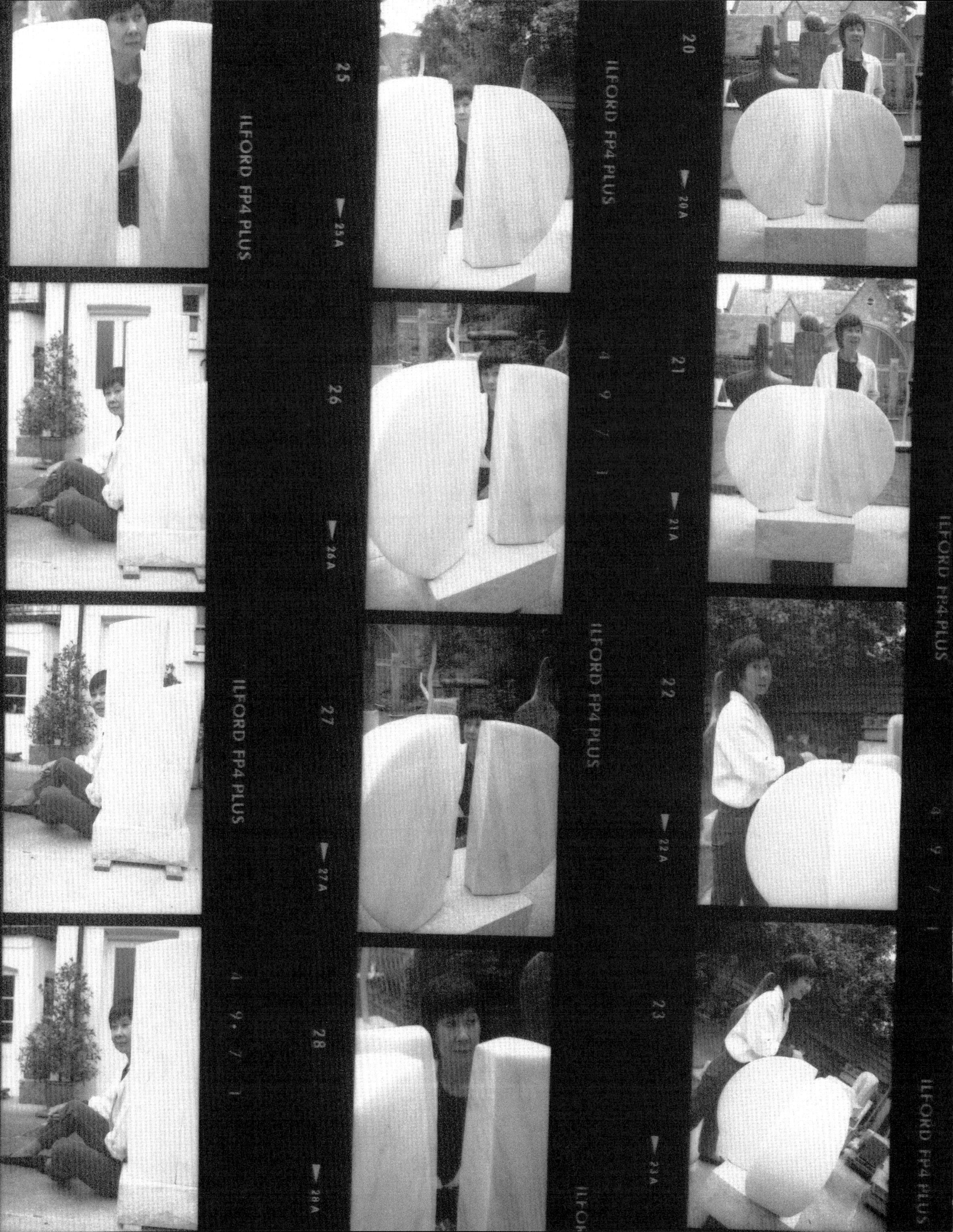

25 ILFORD FP4 PLUS 25A
26 26A
27 ILFORD FP4 PLUS 27A
28 4 9 7 1 28A
20 ILFORD FP4 PLUS 20A
21 4 9 7 1 21A
22 ILFORD FP4 PLUS 22A
23 23A ILFOR
ILFORD FP4 PLUS 4 9 7 1 ILFORD FP4 PLUS

Abi Shapiro

Space, Rhythm and Light in Kim Lim's Work: An Introduction

In 1989 Kim Lim had her portrait taken by photographer Grace Lau in the garden of her home in Camden, north London.[1] The contact sheet (figs 4 and 32) from the shoot shows Lim posing among three of her new stone sculptures. On the left, Lim is seated next to the marble heft of *Kudah* (1989; fig.78) with her legs bent at an angle that echoes the form of the sculpture. With *Segments* (1988) Lim chose to crouch behind the work and peer through the gaps of the stone crescents, each open like a newly peeled orange. And, on the right, the artist drew herself to full standing height over *Source I* (1988), accentuating the right angle of her tall stature with the horizontal carving beneath her.

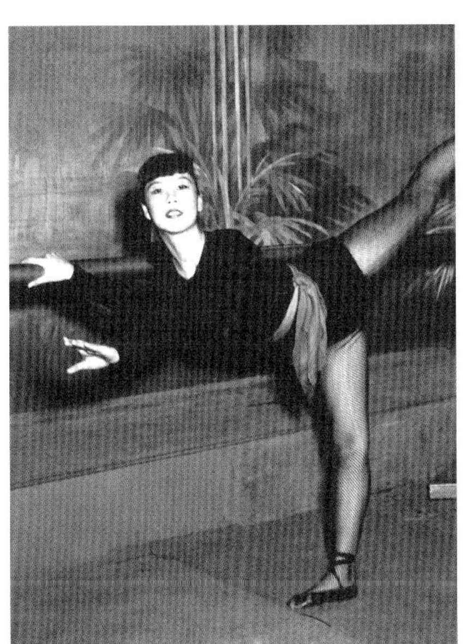

3 Kim Lim in a ballet pose, 1940s
The Estate of Kim Lim

These playful portraits not only convey the human scale of Lim's abstract sculptures, but in them Lim also shows us the relationship between the stone forms and the vital, physical forces the artist's body exerted upon the materials in the carving process. Lim said that in sculpture her main concerns were 'not so much for volume, mass and weight, but rather with form, space, rhythm and light ... For me [light] is no less physical than the others, it is as real as pulse and breathing.'[2]

Light – as a physical presence in sculpture – accentuates the space between forms, which is what Lim seems to be doing by placing her body between and around the sculptures in the photographs. Similarly, by drawing on the bodily reference of 'pulse' and 'breathing', Lim emphasised the value of 'rhythm' in her work. As a teenager in Singapore, Lim trained in ballet (fig.3) before moving to London to study fine art at St Martin's School of Art (known today as Central Saint Martins). This formative love of dance may have been a catalyst for her engagement with themes of rhythm, music and movement that accounts for the visceral appeal many find in her work.

Barbara Hepworth, a near contemporary of Lim's, also understood this kind of calibration of the viewer's body with the artist's body in the presence of an abstract sculpture. Hepworth said, 'you can't make a sculpture, in my opinion, without involving your body. You move and you feel and you breathe and you touch. The spectator is the same. His body is involved too.'[3]

4 Contact sheet of Kim Lim c.1989. with **Kudah** (1989) (left); **Segments** (1988) (right)
The Estate of Kim Lim

That both artists draw on the rhythmic life force of breath to understand this triangulation between sculpture, viewer and artist concretises the embodied encounter of the moment where flesh meets stone meets flesh. Like Lim, Hepworth too was fascinated by music and rhythm and saw them as bound up in her treatment of materials and abstraction. But there are more complex questions at stake here regarding the interpretive relationships that arise between the objects of art and artists' bodies, where the often entangled and vexed issues of biography, geography and identity lurk.

Today, as critical questions are asked of 20th-century Western Eurocentric narratives of modernism and its legacies, these concerns also orbit Lim's legacy, as they do for other artists marginalised by dominant art histories. It is important to consider: what does it mean for Lim to be visible again now? What kinds of questions does this raise about the exclusionary mechanisms of the M/modernist canon? And how do we reappraise Lim's legacy today in a climate where 'difference' remains a contested territory? As several of the authors explore in this publication, Lim's hybrid British-Singaporean-Chinese identity equally enriches and complicates how we understand her work. Their texts suggest that these challenges don't necessarily require resolution; instead they productively trouble assumptions about the neat alignment of identity and geography. As these authors note, Lim herself was well aware that in the overdetermination of her identity as *only* a diasporic artist, her work is reduced within a biographical framework that ignores the social and historical contexts in which she worked and to which she contributed.

In their chapter in this publication, Joleen Loh and Adele Tan, curators at National Gallery Singapore, explore the presence of Asia in Lim's work. They consider Lim's regular trips to Singapore to visit family, and the exhibition of her work there between the 1960s and 1980s. Weaving in discussions of some of the key works in the National Gallery Singapore's collection, the authors discuss alternative ways to contextualise Lim's multi-faceted heritage without being beholden to the centre and peripheries of British art canons. Elsewhere, Joleen Loh has written about Lim's travels across Asia and the artist's use of documentary photography; Loh argues that both influenced Lim's approach to abstraction, but also that these reference points must alter the kinds of art historical engagement we need to make with Lim's work.[4] Tan and Loh remind us that the multiplicity and visibility of Lim's legacies in different geographies and historical contexts can and should foster diverse interpretations.

It is important to note that Lim's visibility was not always limited but rather seemed to oscillate above and below the canonical parapet. Lim enjoyed what can be described as 'art-world success' during her lifetime in Britain and Singapore with a substantial record of exhibitions and representation in significant museum collections and commercial gallery displays. Yet after her death in 1997, only a few notable exhibitions took place: in 1999 at Camden Arts

Centre in London, where a monographic exhibition was held of her stone and print works from the 1970s to the 1990s, and a tribute exhibition at Singapore Art Museum. A gaping stretch of 15 years followed with barely any institutional exposure until a display of Lim's carvings opened at The New Arts Centre at Roche Court Sculpture Park in Salisbury in 2014. As Hammad Nasar discusses in his chapter here, since 2018 Lim's work has begun to feature more prominently in major group survey exhibitions and publications about post-war British art – a space where women of the Global Majority have been particularly absent.

The exhibition at The Hepworth Wakefield, which accompanies this publication, will be the first retrospective to bring together work from across Kim Lim's entire career spanning 1959 to 1997.[5] Not only offering a comprehensive survey of almost 40 years of Lim's practice, both exhibition and publication explore her practice within the context of modern art histories. This volume brings together contributions from key interlocutors of Lim's work, including scholars, curators and those involved in the artist's Estate. Together, they explore in depth the range of Lim's thematic and material engagements, while maintaining a clear focus on the urgent issues at stake in recuperating her legacy as a British-Singaporean artist.

This recent resurfacing of Lim's work may be due to a combination of academic and market forces: long overdue attention is slowly being given to artists with heritage from the Global Majority, coupled with a revived interest in mid-century abstract sculpture. Academic research has also fuelled Lim's visibility, thanks to key scholars such as Joleen Loh and Wenny Teo, as well as research projects like *London, Asia* that explored critical questions about Asian diasporic artists in Britain and the entanglement of local and global art histories.[6]

Another important research project from the last decade was the *Black Artists and Modernism* project, which tracked the work of under-represented artists with African, Asian, Caribbean and MENA-region heritage in UK public art collections. Researchers audited a sample of collections to collate data on those artists born, raised, working or studying in the UK whose work was acquired between 1900 and 2016.[7] In this data set, Kim Lim was the second most collected artist, and the most collected female artist. When the audit of the sample was updated for acquisitions made between 2017 and 2022, Lim remained in the top five most collected artists, with 93 works in the audited collections.[8] Today, we know Lim is represented in 14 UK public art collections and seven international public collections including museums in Japan, Singapore, Hong Kong, the United Arab Emirates, Belgium and the United States. Discussions of Lim's work can be found now in podcasts, magazines and international art fairs, signalling her belated arrival in more mainstream arenas.[9]

Kim Lim's story is one of courage and tenacity. Born in Singapore in 1936 to Chinese middle-class parents, Lim spent her childhood between the city of her birth (prior to independence) and the states of Penang and Malacca in Malaya (Malaysia). Her father, Lim Koon Teck, was a magistrate and her mother, Betty Lim, the daughter of a banking family. After the family was trapped in Malaya during the Japanese invasion and occupation between 1941 and 1945, they eventually returned to Singapore. Lim was restless there, recalling the city as a 'difficult place to be creative in'[10] where her 'exposure to art was limited'.[11]

In 1954 Kim moved to London to study at St Martin's School of Art, where she met fellow artist and lifelong friend Tess Jaray and studied under Anthony Caro and Elisabeth Frink. At the time Caro was still making figurative work, and despite his own practice becoming heavily abstract soon after, he disparaged Lim's initial non-figurative experiments. In 1956, at Frink's encouragement, Lim transferred to the Slade School of Fine Art where she pursued sculpting and printmaking. Tutors Anthony Gross and Stanley Jones particularly encouraged Lim's experimentation in printmaking with abstract forms, where she excelled in lithography, screenprint and etching (fig.5).

Lim comfortably moved between printmaking and sculpture with deft material and technical awareness. In screenprints such as *King, Queen, Pawn* (1960; fig.6) and *Head* (1960; fig.8) Lim translated abstract forms between two and three dimensions (figs 6 and 11). The sculptures not only bear the same titles as the prints but they share clear formal similarities. Printmaking remained a key part of Lim's work until her death, a practice she conceived as of 'equal importance' to her sculpture.[12] Julia Farrer, a friend of the artist, articulated this relationship, stating that the 'fluidity of lithography provided a bridge between drawing and sculpture and the physicality of the woodcut and the copper plate etching linking sculpture back to drawing' (figs 13, 14).[13]

Early sculptures from this period at the Slade include *Muse* (1959; fig.10), *Head* (1959; fig.11), *Kiss* (1959; fig.38), *Narcissus* (1959; fig.12) and *Chess Piece I* (1960; fig.9). They convey Lim's focus on the compositional relationship between largely abstract forms that nevertheless are still underpinned by lingering traces of the figure. Lim's admiration of Constantin Brancusi's ability to bring presence to space with his streamlined abstract sculptures can be seen in her work at this time.

In her chapter for this book, Ming Tiampo explores the formative years of Lim's education at the Slade in the late 1950s. Tiampo suggests Lim's burgeoning formal interest in negative space was also imbricated in the artist's symbolic engagement with non-Western cultures, describing these 'spaces in between ... both as formal elements to be manipulated, and also as geographic and cultural spaces to be explored'. Tiampo unpicks Lim's minimalist approach to abstraction not so much as a 'reduction' in relation

5 **Untitled**, 1958 screenprint on paper, 56 × 59 cm (22 × 23 in) The Estate of Kim Lim

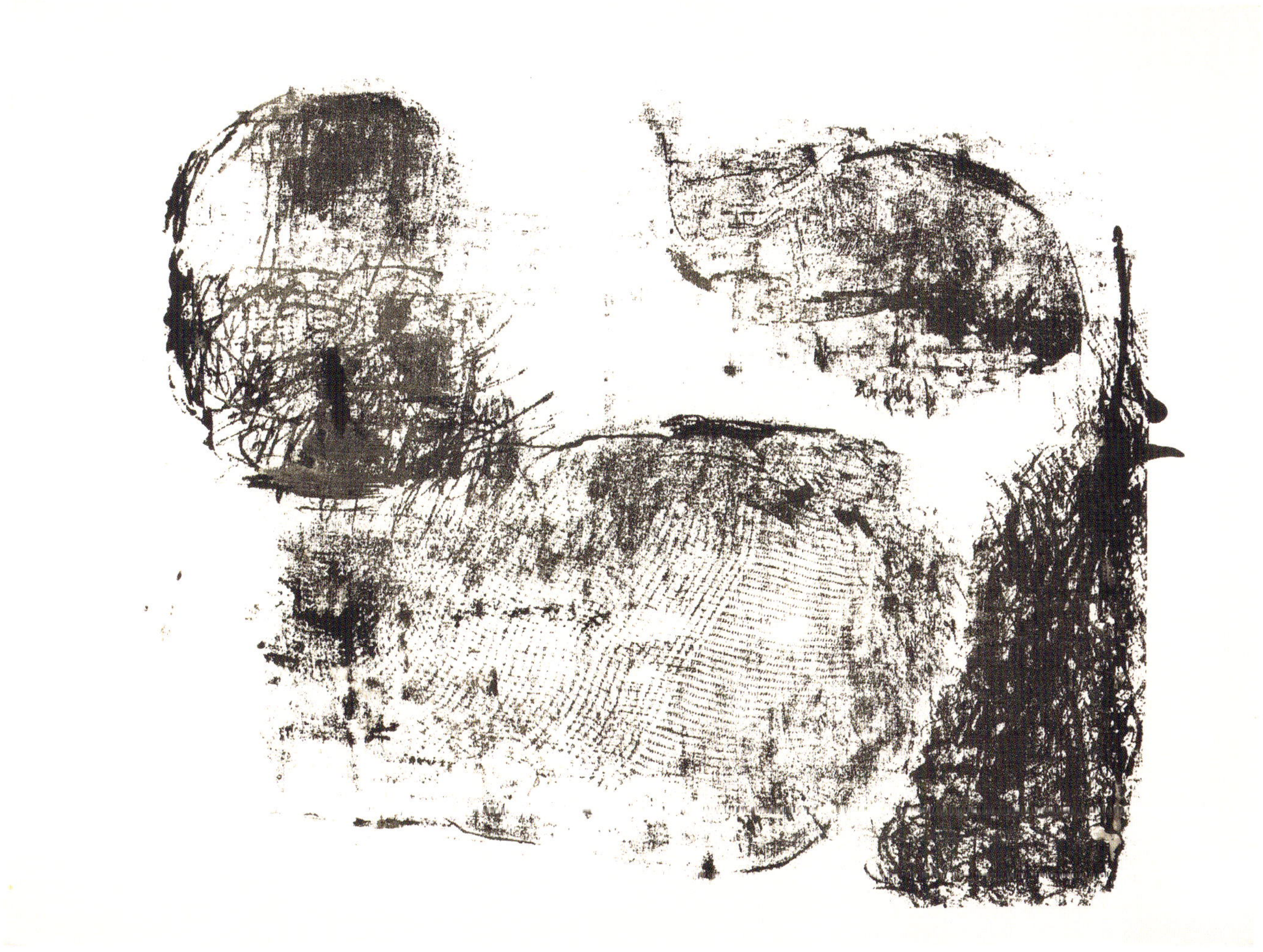

6 **King, Queen, Pawn**, 1960 screenprint on paper, 55 × 69·8 cm (22 × 27 in) The Estate of Kim Lim

7 **King, Queen, Pawn**, 1959 wood, in three parts, 94 × 67 × 46 cm (37 × 26 × 18 in) Collection of Chong Huai Seng and Ning Chong, Singapore

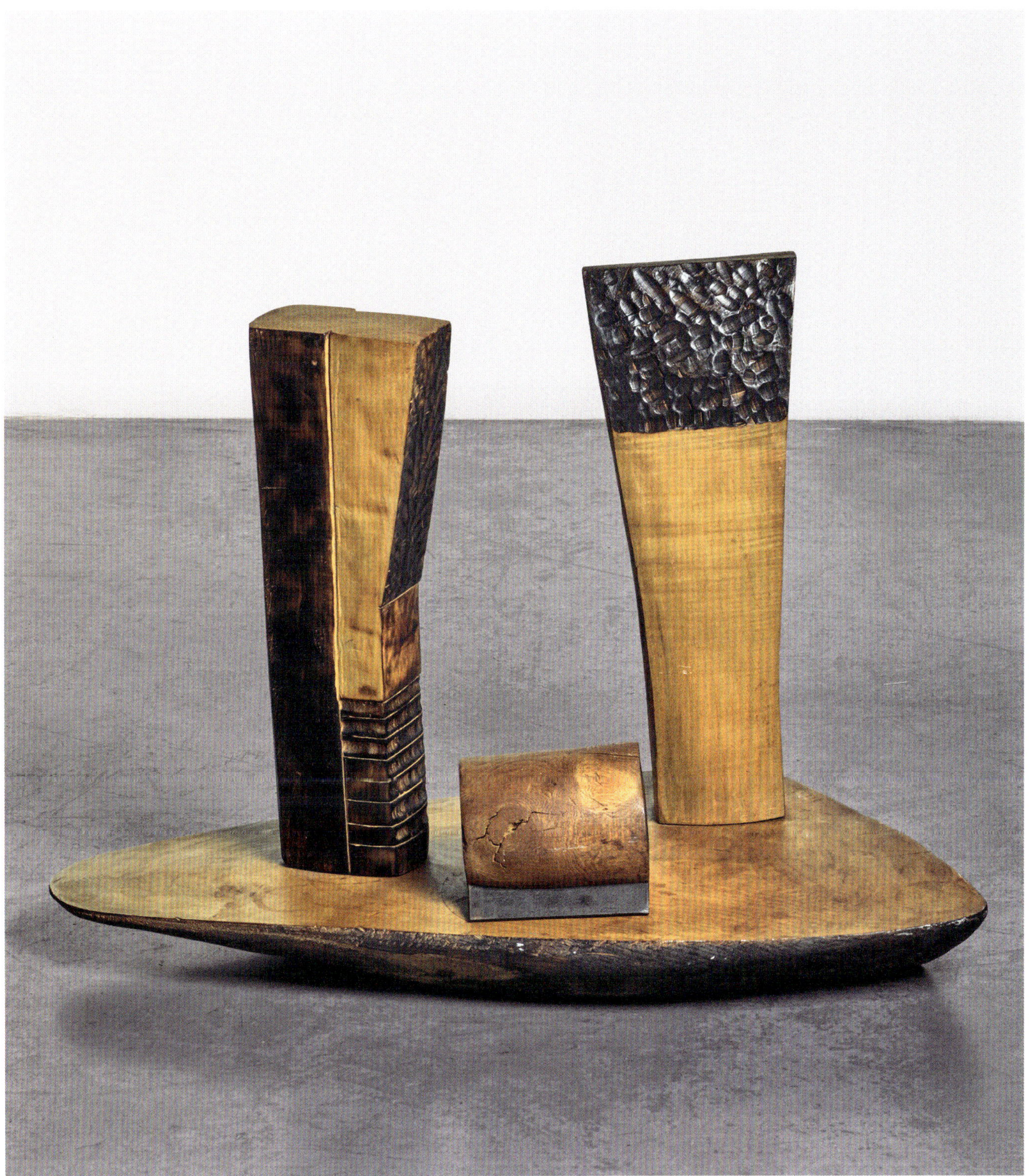

8 **Head**, 1960 screenprint on paper, 53·5 × 77·6 cm (21 × 30 in) The Estate of Kim Lim

9 **Chess Piece I**, 1960 wood, 55 × 45 × 34 cm (22 × 18 × 13 in) The Estate of Kim Lim

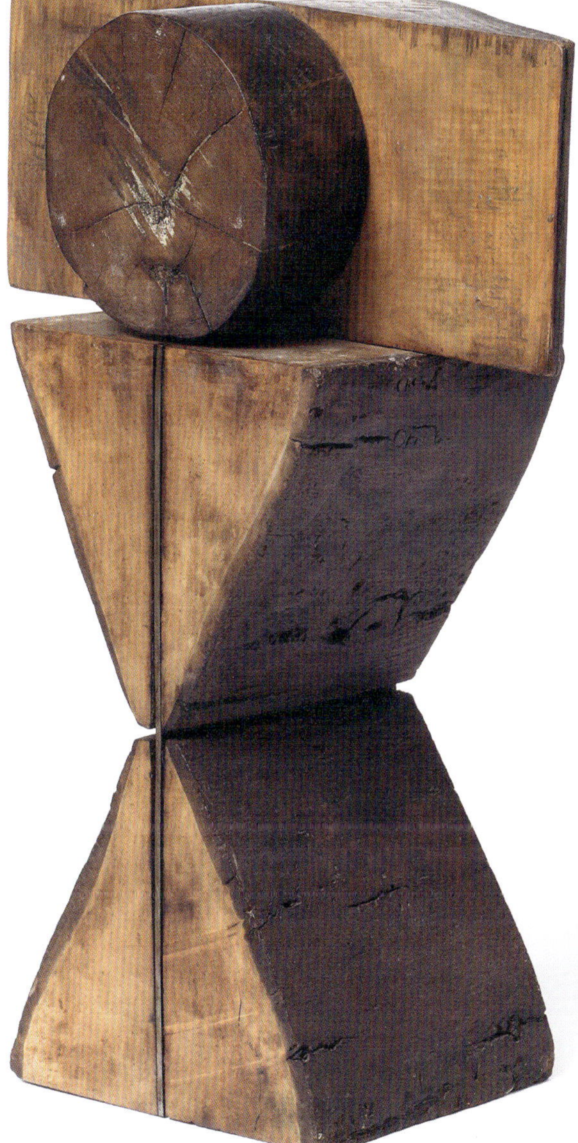

10 **Muse**, 1959 walnut and cherry, 45 × 16 × 16 cm (18 × 6 × 6 in)
The Estate of Kim Lim

11 **Head**, 1959 stone, 19 × 12 × 15 cm (7 × 5 × 6 cm)
The Estate of Kim Lim

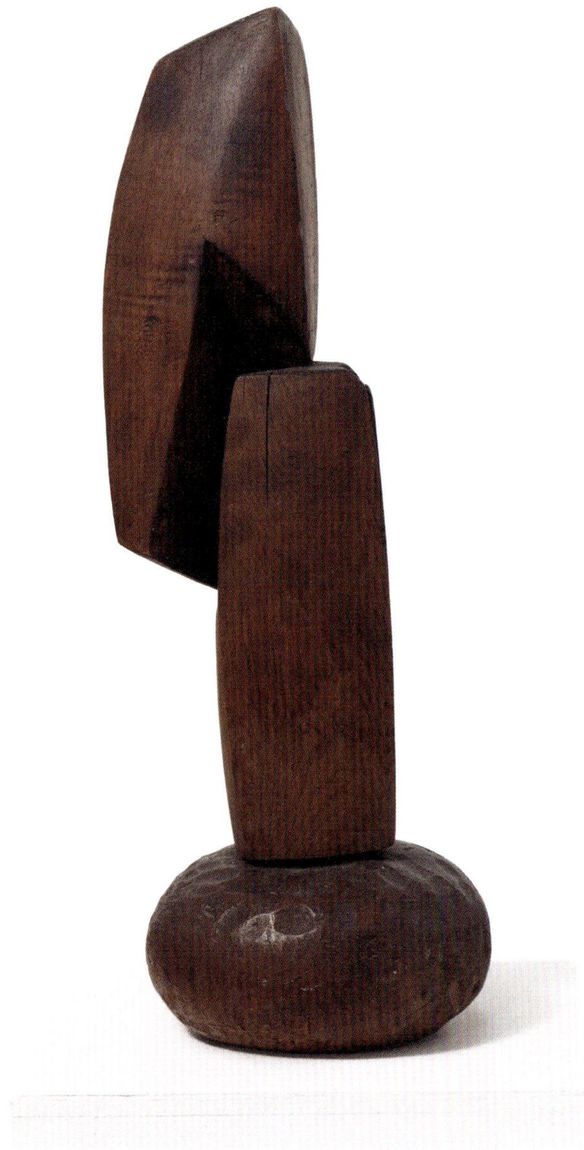

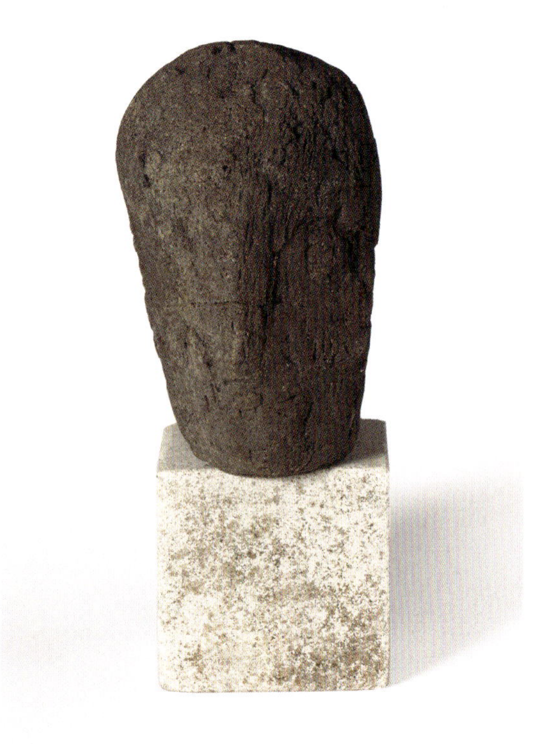

12 **Narcissus**, 1959 bronze, 61·6 × 52 × 52 cm (24 × 20 × 20 in) The Estate of Kim Lim

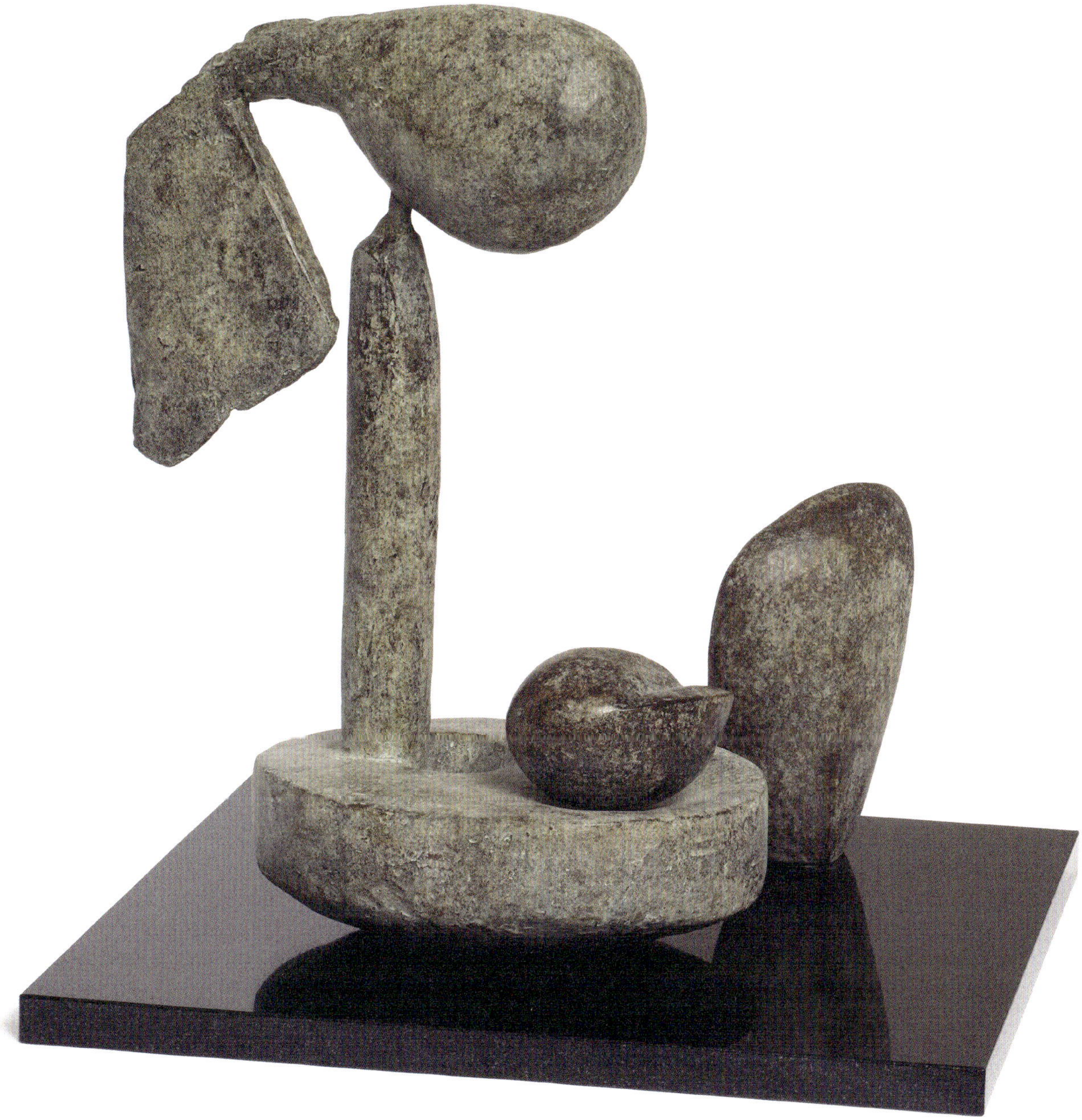

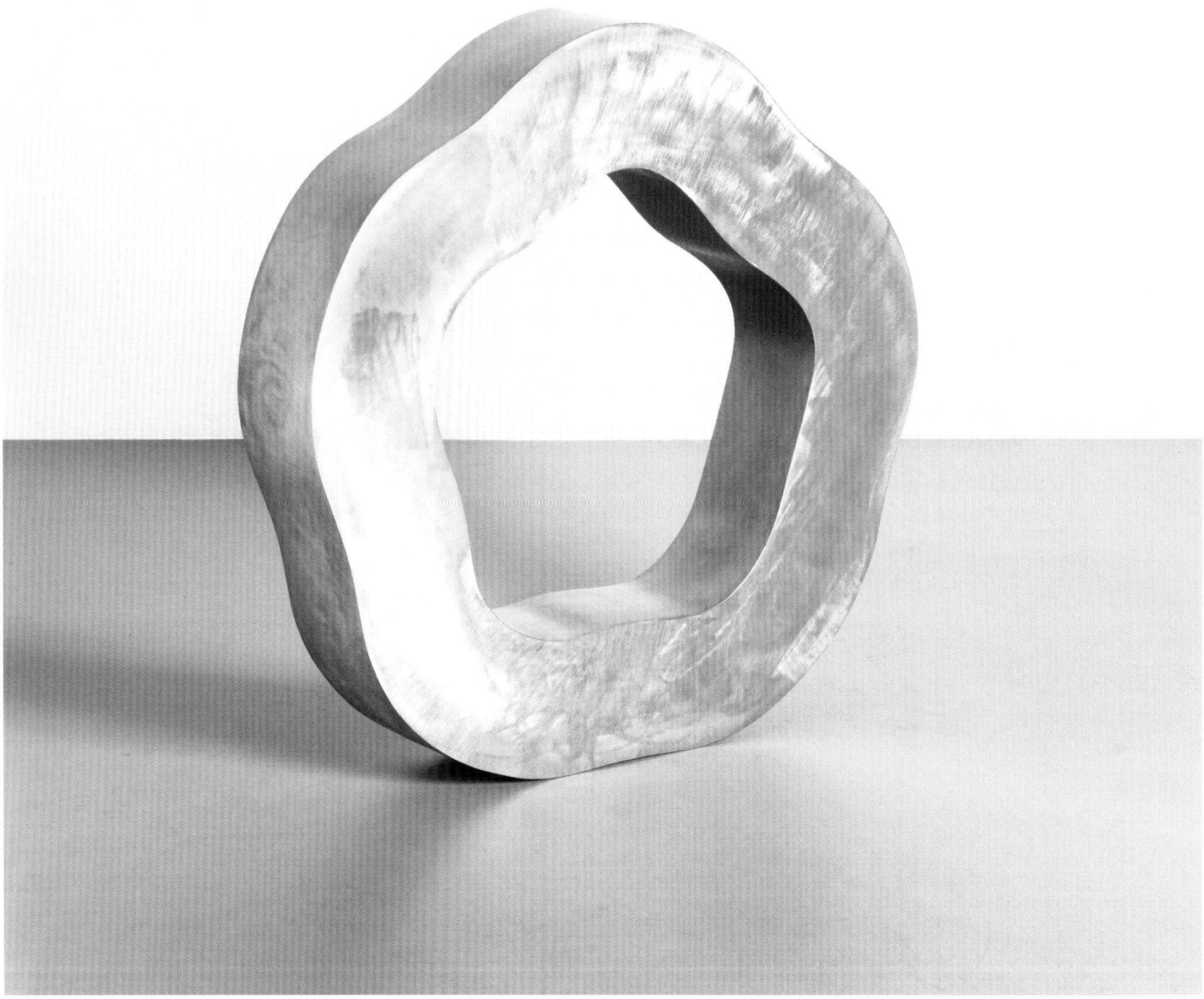

13 **Ring**, 1972 stainless steel, 66 × 66 × 12·7 cm (26 × 5 × 5 in) The Estate of Kim Lim

14 **'Free Forms'**, 1969 etching on paper, 51 × 51 cm (20 × 20 in) The Estate of Kim Lim

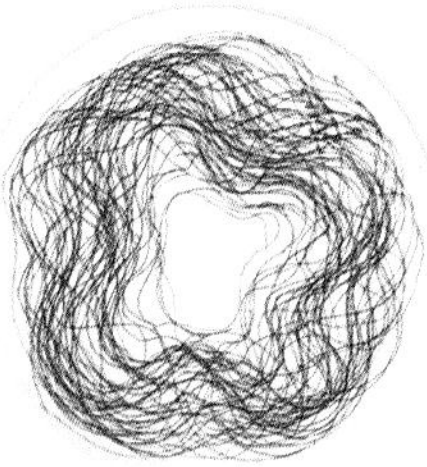

15 Kim Lim and William Turnbull playing chess, *c.*1970 The Estate of Kim Lim

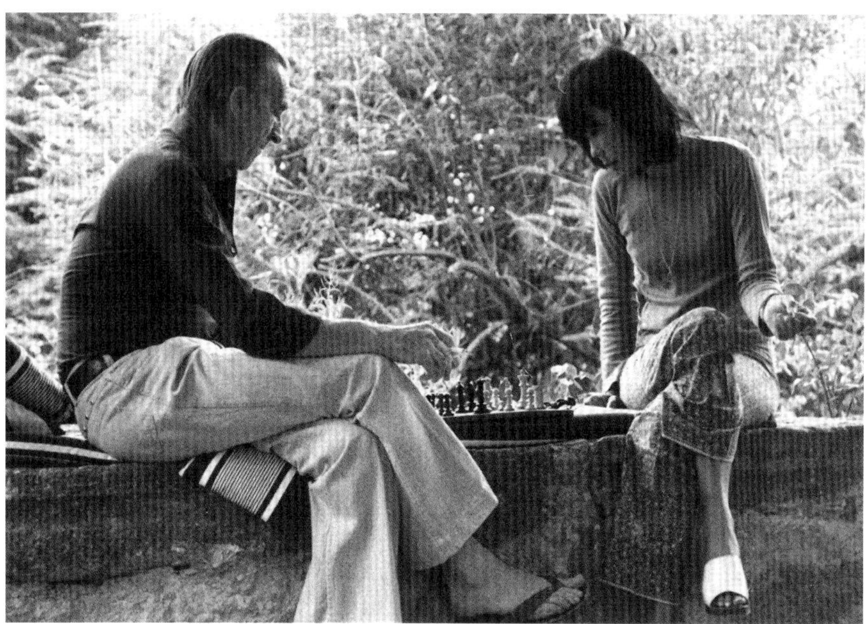

to representation, but rather as a simplification of the 'essence of form' and the communication of embodied experience.

After graduating in 1960, Lim rented a studio in a disused chemistry workshop in north London which gave her the freedom to experiment with new materials. Sculptures such as *Samurai* (1961; fig.16), *Caryatid* (1961; fig.17) and *Ronin* (1963; fig.18) were made from found pieces of scrap wood arranged in modular configurations, relying on the juxtaposition of forms with minimal intervention into the material to emphasise its 'natural state'.[14] Lim said: 'I used to go to wood yards ... and buy kind of off-cuts and things ... I was very interested in assembling. I mean I'd given up carving in one piece ... so I would take several shapes, carve them up and fix them together.'[15] Lim's work has yet to be discussed in relation to techniques of assemblage or collage in the context of British art – an approach popular in North America at the time. It would, for example, be interesting to consider Lim in dialogue with assemblage artists such as Louise Nevelson (who exhibited in London in 1963 at Hanover Gallery – a show Lim likely would have seen).

In 1957 Lim met Scottish sculptor William Turnbull and they married in 1960. Not long after, they moved to a large home in Camden, north London, where each had their own studio. Two sons, Alex and Johnny, followed in the subsequent years. Connections between the two artists' work have not been given much attention despite a number of formal and material similarities (especially in the 1960s). This is understandable as Turnbull's legacy once

16 **Samurai**, 1961 wood, 104·8 × 66 × 60·3 cm (41 × 26 × 24 in) Arts Council Collection, Southbank Centre, London

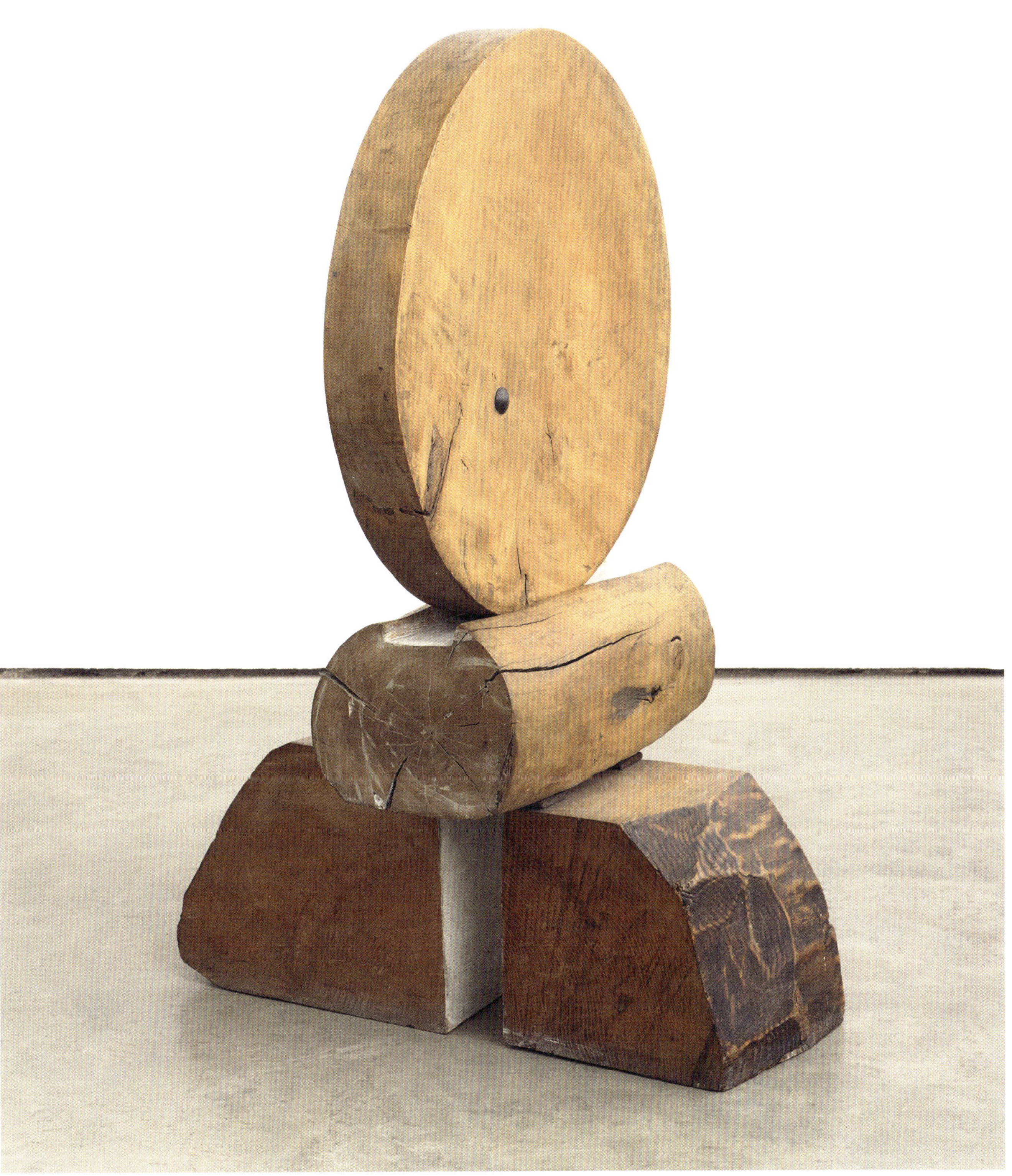

17 **Caryatid**, 1961 wood and stone, 98·5 × 45 × 20 cm (37 × 18 × 8 in) Private Collection

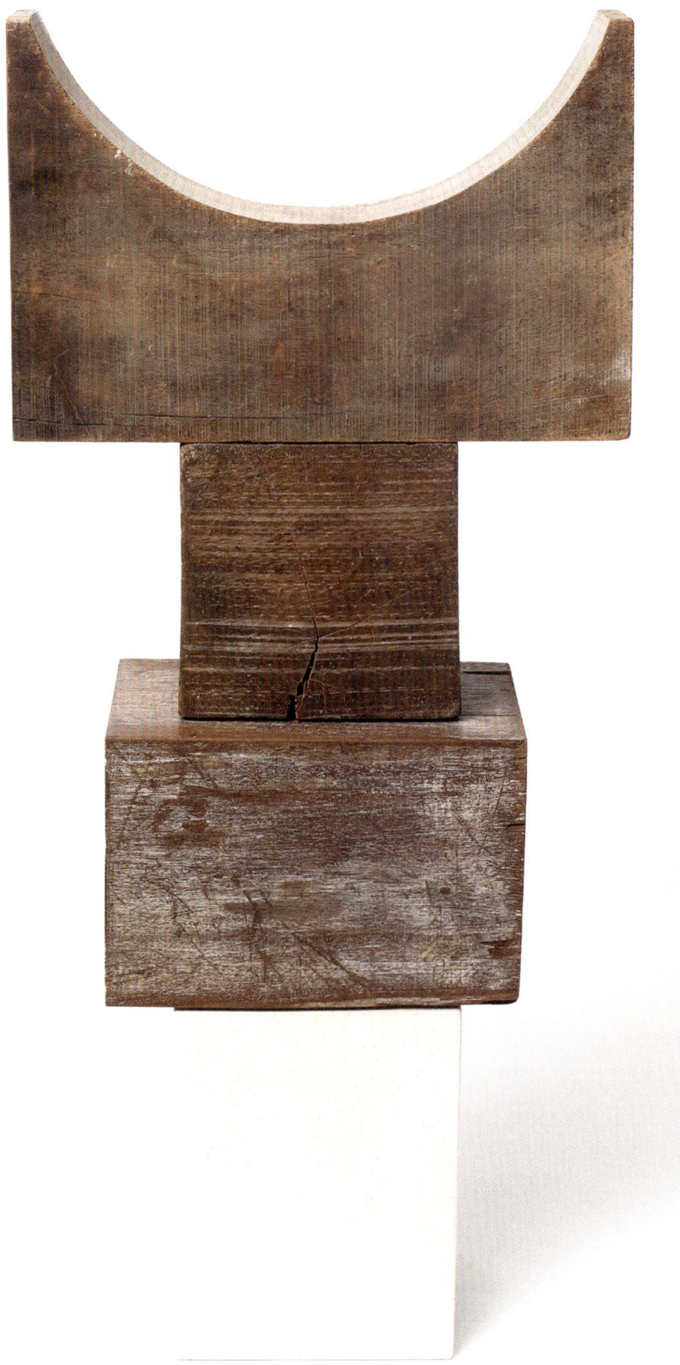

18 **Ronin**, 1963 wood and metal in five parts, 30·6 × 77 × 29 cm (12 × 30 × 11 in) The Estate of Kim Lim

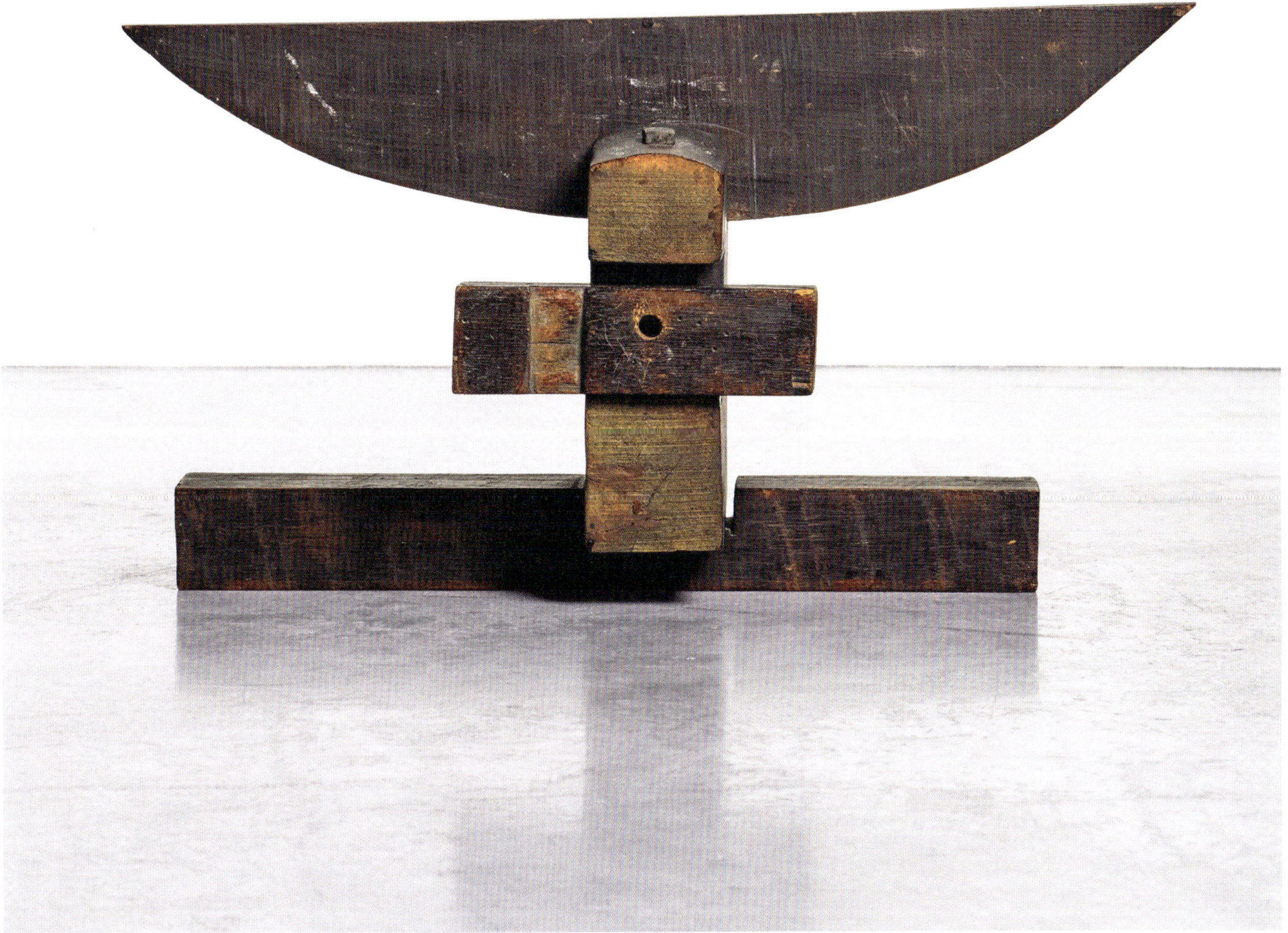

19 Kim Lim, *c.*1950s The Estate of Kim Lim

overshadowed Lim's; even in the press for her own work she was sometimes merely referred to as his 'wife'. Yet, as their son Alex says: 'they both influenced each other ... they had a lot of respect for each other as artists, and when you travel together frequently, you're both going to be referencing elements of the same thing, taking the influences into your work and observing how the other person interprets the same thing.' [16]

The two artists travelled together extensively from 1962 onwards, going to Europe, North America and Asia regularly. Several authors in this publication, including Tan, Loh and Tiampo, examine the way Lim's travels – what the artist called her 'main art education' – to museums, architectural and archaeological sites were generative for her work (fig.19). Titles of sculptures and prints, for example, contain references to places Lim and Turnbull visited. We see artworks with the Malaysian titles *Trengannu* and *Borneo*, and references to Chinese caves in the *Dunhuang* prints (fig.20), as well as titles borrowing names and characters from Greek and Japanese mythology, such as *Samurai*, (fig.16), *Narcissus* (fig.12), *Minerva*, *Centaur II* (fig.21) and *Pegasus* (fig.22).

As Lim's style and minimalist approach to form cohered, the artist had her first solo exhibition at Axiom Gallery, London, in 1966. In her chapter, Wenny Teo discusses this key exhibition which suggests not only the maturation of Lim's style in assembling forms in trendy new materials such as steel and colourful painted wood (figs 23 and 24), but also Lim's confidence working on a larger, monumental scale, like her contemporaries the 'New Generation' sculptors David Annesley, Michael Bolus and William Tucker who, like Lim, were all students of Anthony Caro's. Teo analyses in depth the sculpture *Day* (1966; fig.48), which Lim thought to be one of the most successful expressions of her ideas about form and space.

By the late 1960s and early 1970s, Lim's interest in assemblage gave way to a more conceptual approach, working in series to explore repetition and rhythm with movable, modular components. Hammad Nasar examines some of these concerns in his text, discussing the multi-partite series *Intervals* (1973; fig.57), *Link* (1975; figs 30 and 56) and *Interstices* (1977; fig.84) that show Lim's playful and malleable spatial interventions where pieces could be arranged in new configurations according to the space. He considers how seriality and rhythm were bound up in Lim's interest in music, drawing on Lim's works on paper including her lesser-discussed *Paper Cut* works – a body of quasi-sculptural works made with heavy card (figs 25 and 26). In this period, Lim also engaged vivid colours in her sculptures and prints, devising playful interventions for their display. For example, the suite *Discs* comprises 12 brightly hued aquatints, all made in 1972, which were placed back to back and suspended from the ceiling within transparent acrylic cases so they would spin freely in space (figs 27 and 28).

20 **Dunhuang Series II**, 1986 lithograph on paper, 74 × 56 cm (29 × 22 in) The Estate of Kim Lim

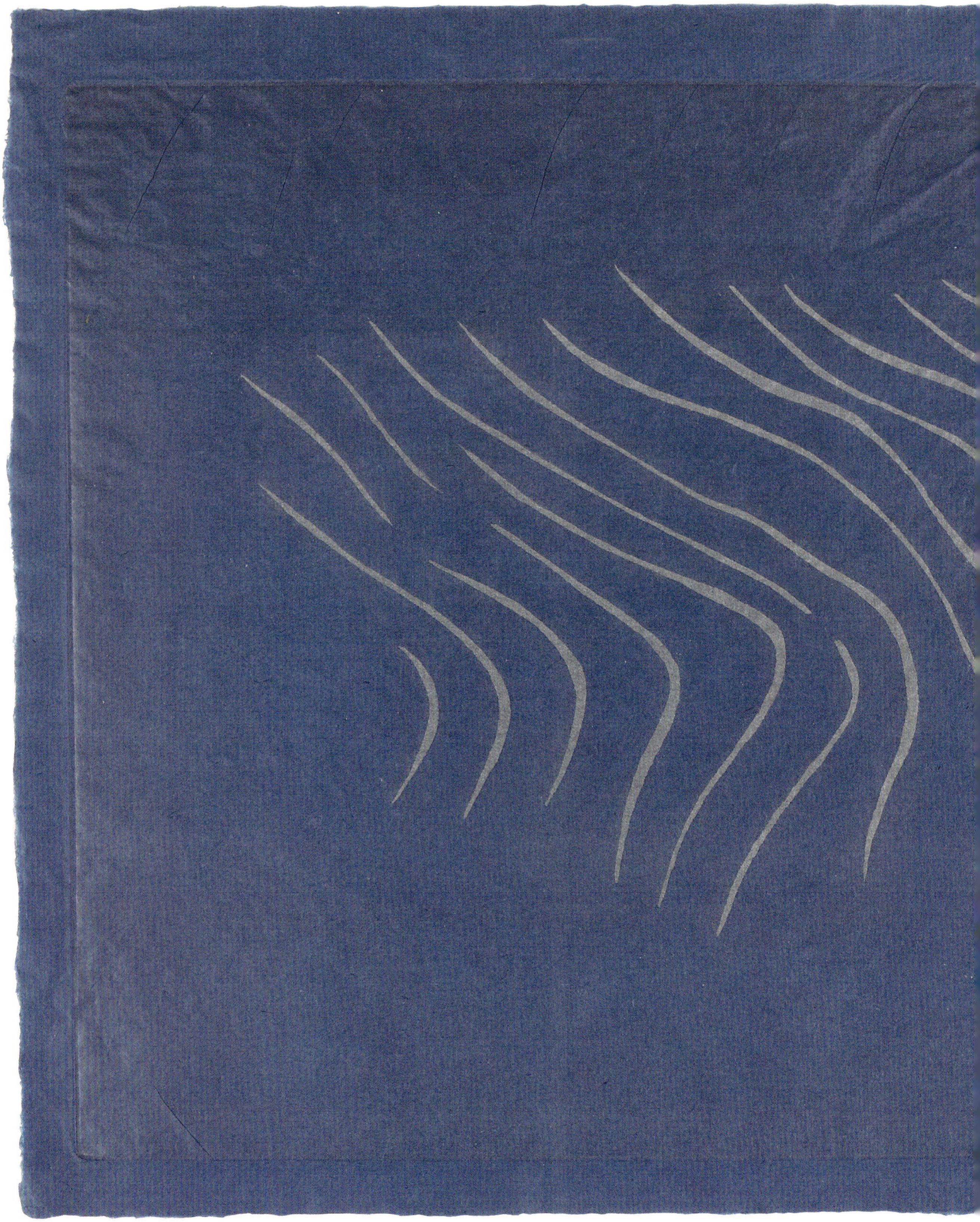

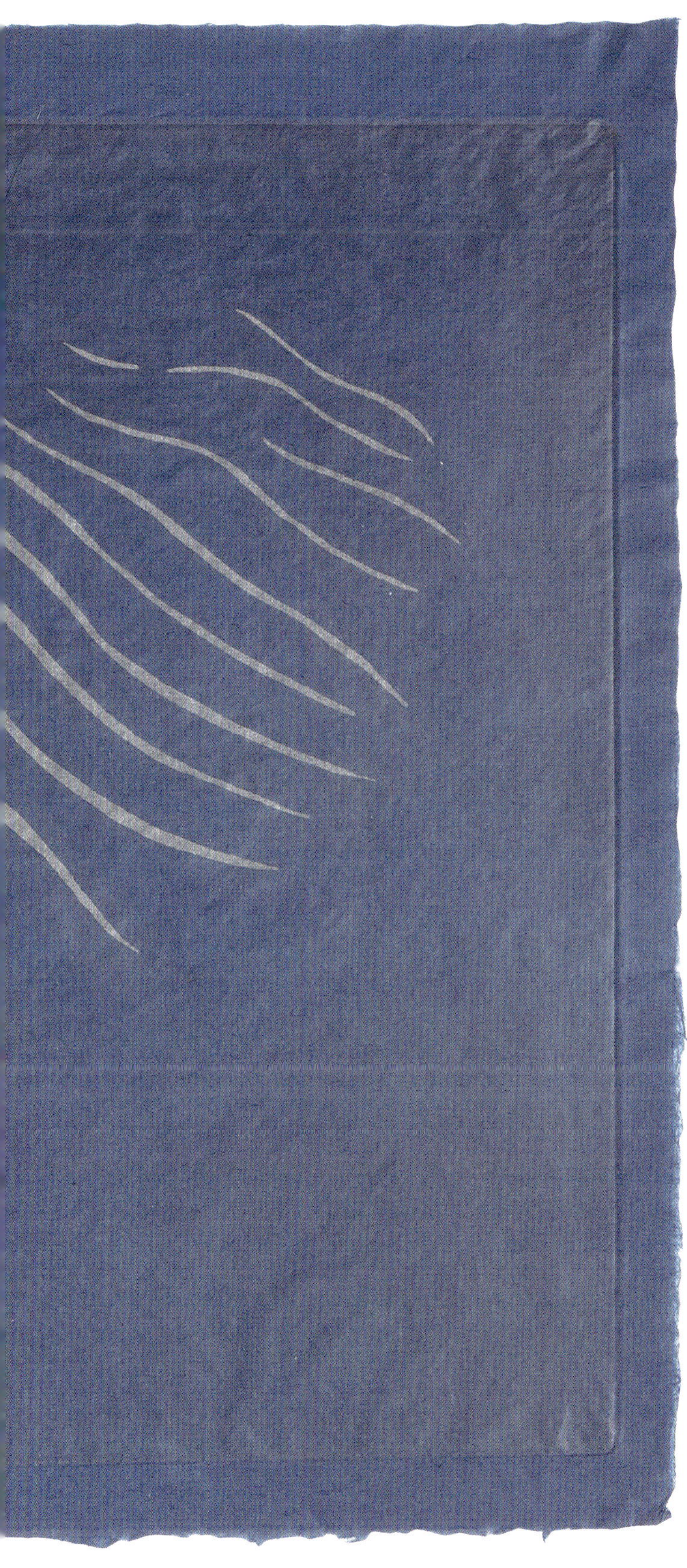

21 **Centaur II**, 1963 bronze, 67 × 16 × 25·5 cm (26 × 6 × 10 in) The Estate of Kim Lim

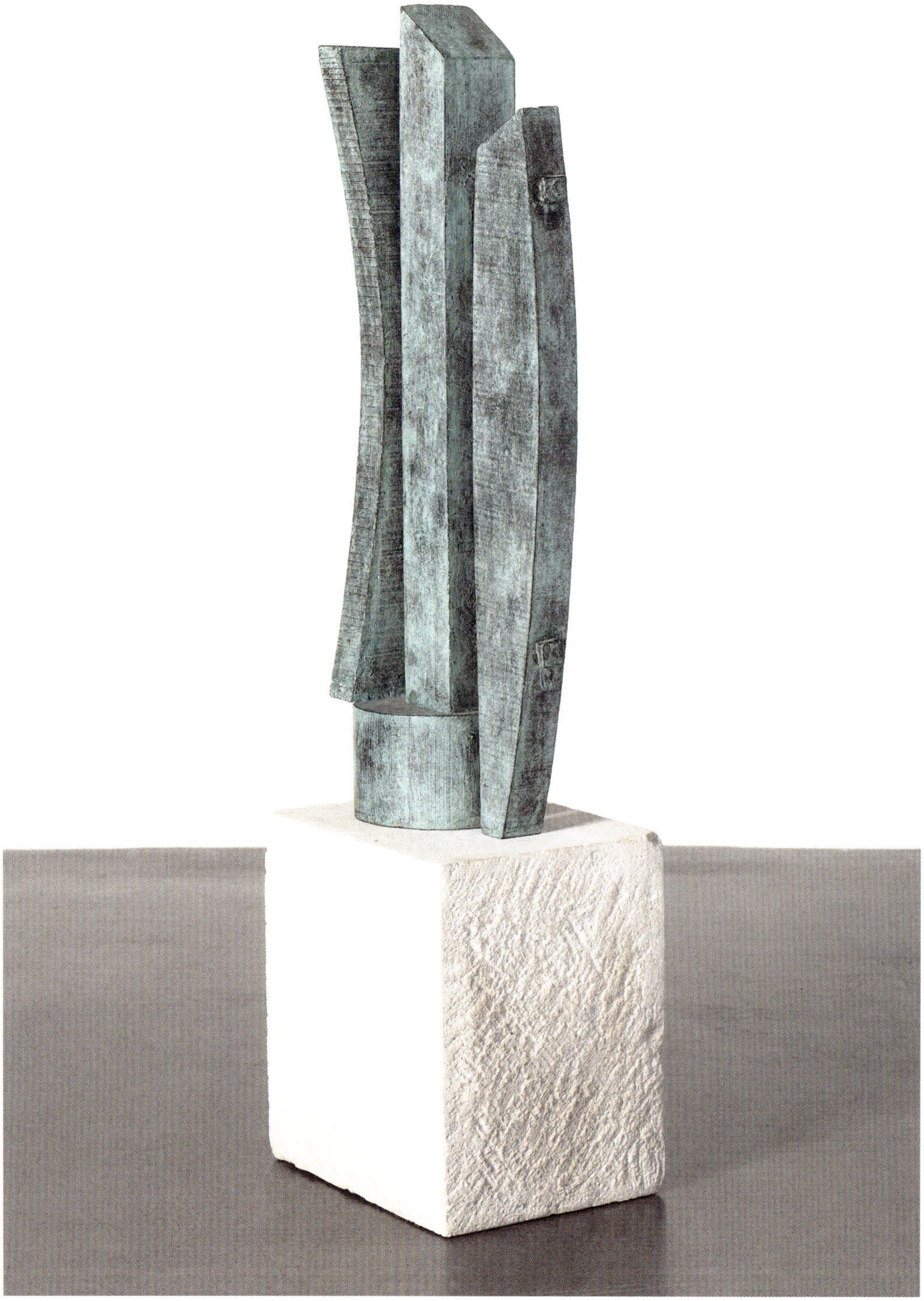

22 **Pegasus**, 1962 bronze, edition of 4 (#1/4), 104 × 51 × 15 cm (41 × 20 × 6 in) The Estate of Kim Lim

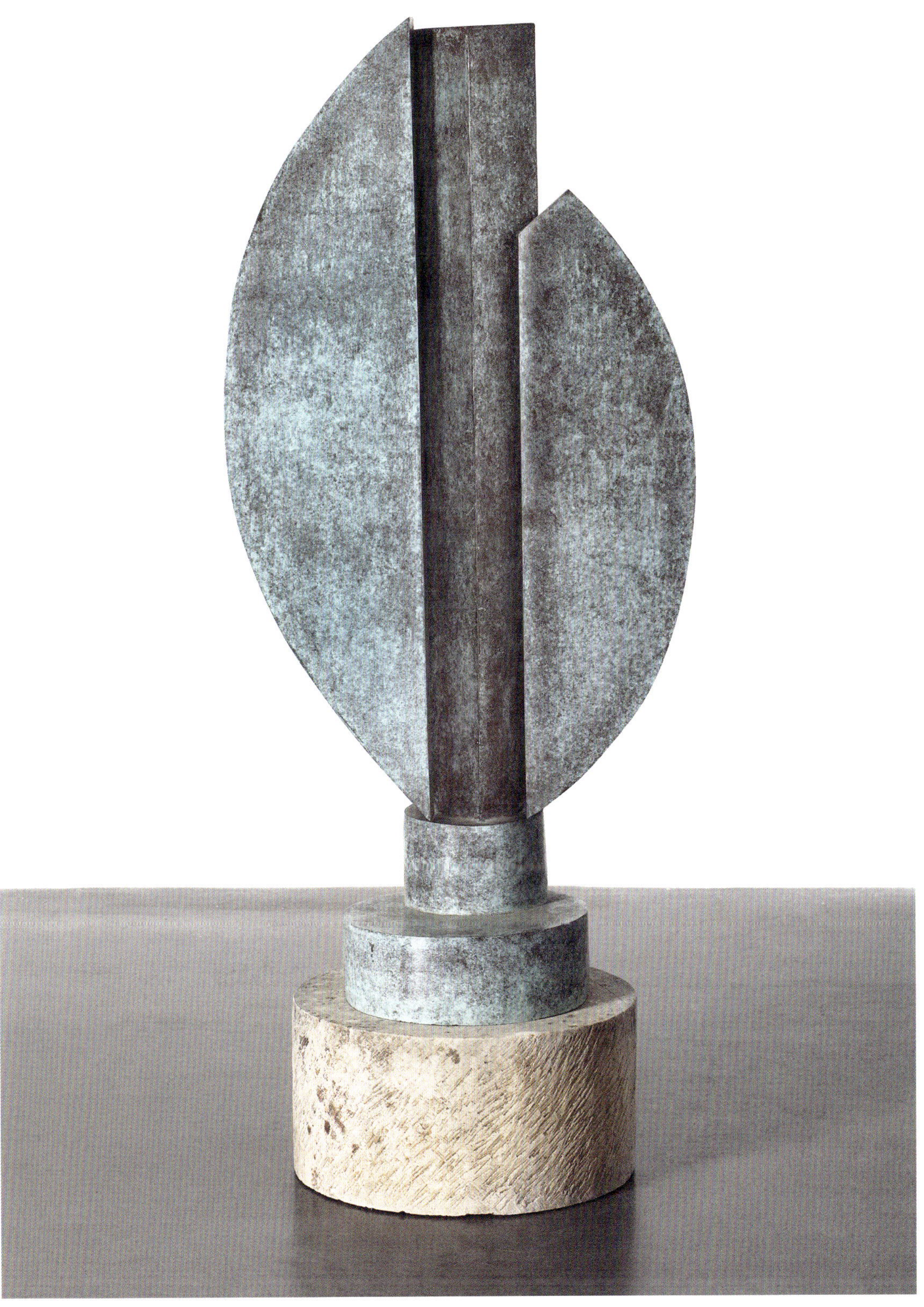

23 **Centaur I**, 1963 painted wood, 67 × 16 × 25·5 cm (27 × 6 × 10 in) The Estate of Kim Lim

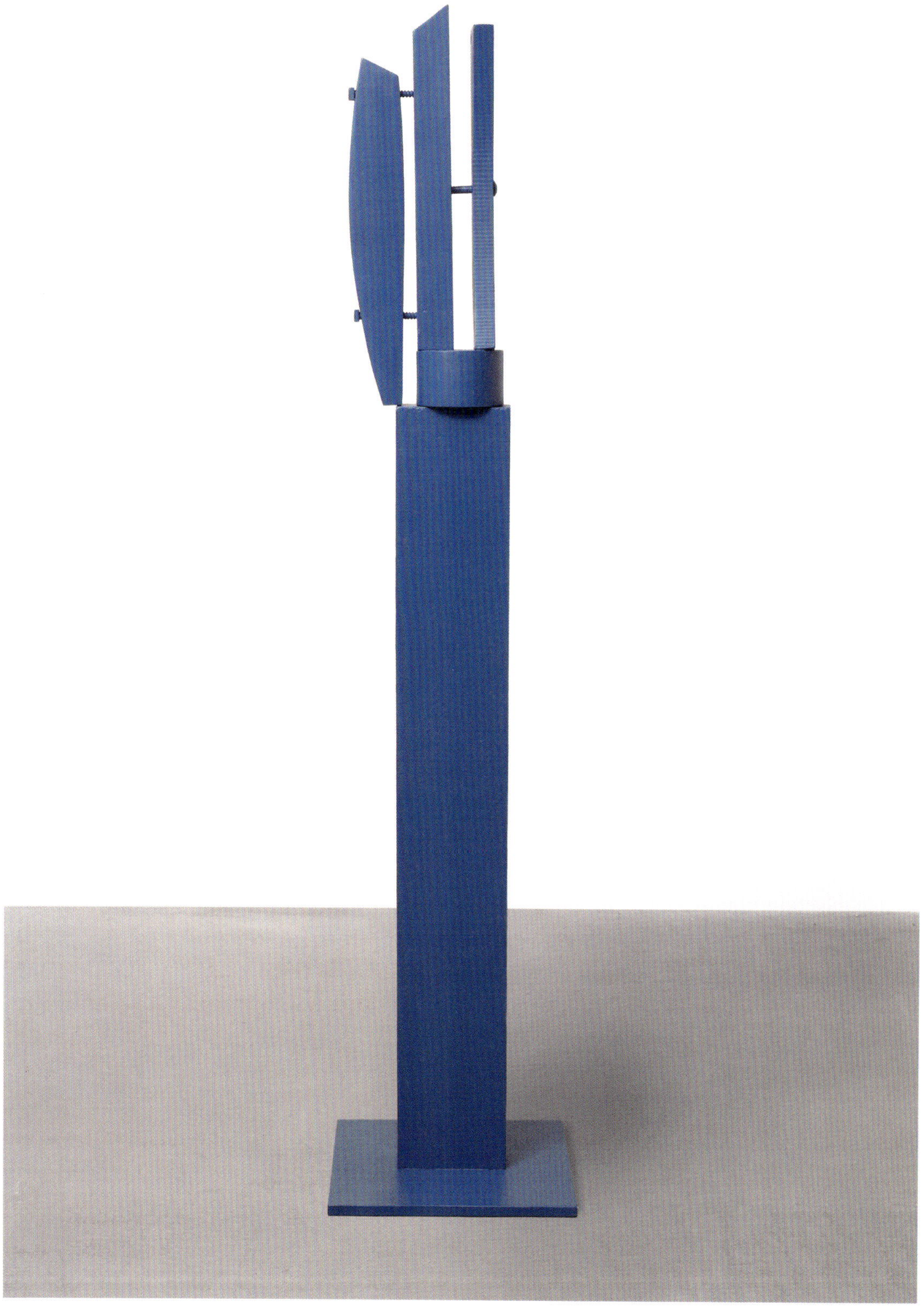

24 **Table**, 1964 painted wood, 51 × 44 × 53 cm (20 × 17 × 21 in) The Estate of Kim Lim

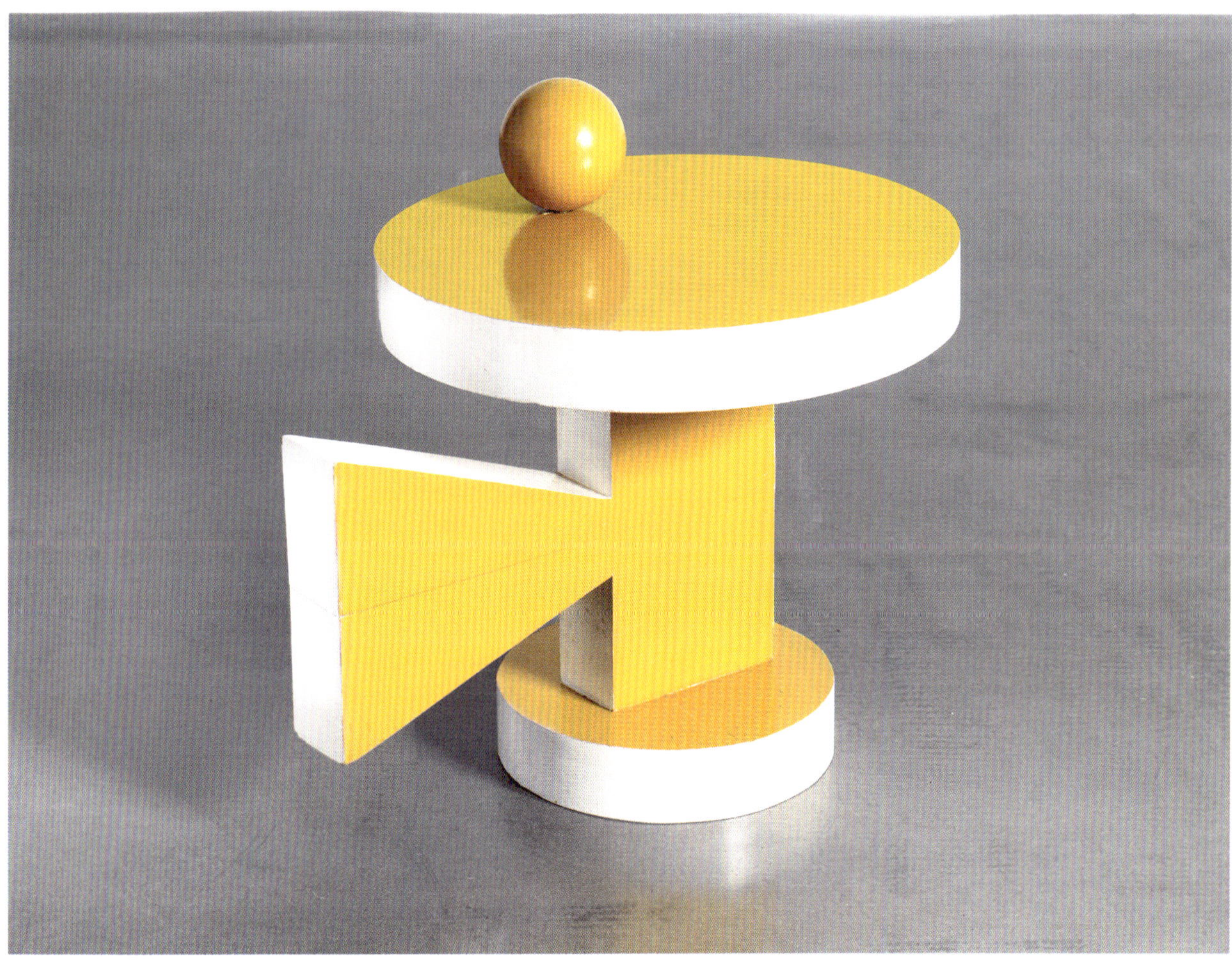

25 **Untitled**, 1976 paper, 45 × 47 cm (18 × 19 in) The Estate of Kim Lim

26 **Untitled**, 1976 paper, 45 × 47 cm (18 × 19 in) The Estate of Kim Lim

27 **Untitled**, 1972 back-to-back aquatint on circle-shaped paper inside circular acrylic (suspended), 52·7 cm (21 in) diameter The Estate of Kim Lim

28 **Untitled**, 1972 back-to-back aquatint on circle-shaped paper inside circular acrylic (suspended), 52·7 cm (21 in) diameter The Estate of Kim Lim

Although Lim's artistic output across her career remained firmly in the realm of abstract forms and she never suggested there was a specific meaning to her work, her practice was happening amid wider social and political shifts. As Wenny Teo notes, Lim had to navigate an art world that wasn't easy if you weren't a white man. Teo discusses the controversies that surrounded Lim's inclusion in the 1977 Hayward Gallery Annual, when Lim was the only woman and the only artist of the Global Majority in the exhibition. In 1978, in an attempt to address the gross imbalance, the Hayward (who openly acknowledged they were giving women preferential treatment) placed Lim on the selection panel consisting of five female artists. In her foreword to the exhibition catalogue, American feminist activist and critic Lucy Lippard wrote, 'it has taken some courage to organise a mixed show while admitting to a bias in favour of women. All-male shows selected by all-male juries have never stated their prejudice so openly.'[17]

While Lim never described herself as a feminist, she didn't shy away from publicly discussing inequality either. In an interview with Sarah Kent, Lim remarked that 'you have to prove yourself in terms of the outside world doubly as a woman'.[18] In 1988 Lim chose to participate in a survey conducted by artist Lorna Green that asked hundreds of women about their experience of being a sculptor in Britain. Green received over three hundred replies from artists of varying generations including Veronica Ryan, Phyllida Barlow, Helen Chadwick and Liliane Lijn. In her response, Lim referred to the 'inequalities' women faced and the fact that juggling studio work and childcare 'was difficult at the time'.[19]

Lim's sudden pivot to carving stone in 1979 was precipitated by seeing her new and old work displayed together at her first survey exhibition at the Roundhouse Gallery in London that same year (fig.31). She showed metal and wooden sculptures as well as prints from the 1960s and 1970s. Reflecting on this shift a few years later, Lim said the exhibition 'made me aware of the pull within myself of organic structured forms. How to incorporate and synthesise these two seemingly opposed elements within one work became the preoccupation and starting point for the recent stone sculptures.'[20]

In the 17 years that followed, Lim made bold, totemic sculptures from marble, Portland stone and granite, increasingly attracted to sensory, elemental forms derived from nature that she described as 'things I have seem [sic.] and experienced and heard' (fig.29).[21] Carvings such as *Wind-Stone* (1992; fig.33), *Column P* (1984; fig.35) and *Column* (1984; fig.34) are incised with rhythmic, striated grooves – a characteristic typical of Lim's works in the late 1980s and 1990s that appears in prints and collages such as *III, IV, V* (1993; fig.36) and *Untitled* (1995; fig.37). Lim said, 'I put lines on the surface of stone to give a kind of rhythmic structure to the piece. I use the lines as

29 Kim Lim, draft of interview with 'J.M.', date not known The Estate of Kim Lim

J.M. Sometimes you think of people getting their inspiration from a concept or from natural forms, or from some influence of from some starting point. Are you aware of any just looking back?

K.L. It is difficult to pinpoint that which germinates the process of thinking or working in a certain way. All I can say is the natural world, things I have seem and experienced and heard are potential source material - all grist for the mill. Because the work is termed non-figurative it does not necessarily mean it is not related to the natural environment. Something I read somewhere said it very succinctly -

visual reality is not necessarily visual verisimilitude

I sometimes make drawings of structures of all kinds - plants, trees, shells, rock, walls, skeletal structures

a method of leading the eye round and creating a kind of composition.'[22] Lim worked until the mid-1990s, when illness impeded carving and printmaking. The artist died of cancer in London in 1997.

Bianca Chu, writer, curator and special advisor to the Estate of Kim Lim, has written her text for this publication in dialogue with Lim's two sons, Alex and Johnny, while all three travelled across Asia. As a trio, they make up Lim's Estate, and in her text Chu examines the various kinds of labour involved in caring for an artist's legacy. This text offers a rare insight into the private work of Estates – what Chu calls a 'web' where 'relationships, experiences, memories, knowledge bases, actions, objects and materials converge'. She outlines some of the ways knowledge about an artist's life forms and the subsequent effects this has on their work. Her text explores the parallel concerns of devotion, sound and silence in both Lim's and the Estate's work, in a convergence of creativity and subjectivity. As such, this reminds us of the responsibility of the interlocutors of artists' legacies – be it estates, critics, curators, researchers or anyone else – to be sensitive to the position from which they speak in order to consider what is not only at stake in their interpretation but in the context in which their interventions are received.

In this dynamic moment of (re)telling and (re)exhibiting Modern British sculpture, we must continue to seek meaningful ways to deconstruct and reconstruct modernist narratives to tell stories on their own terms and not

30 Kim Lim with her printing press and **Link II** (1975), no date The Estate of Kim Lim

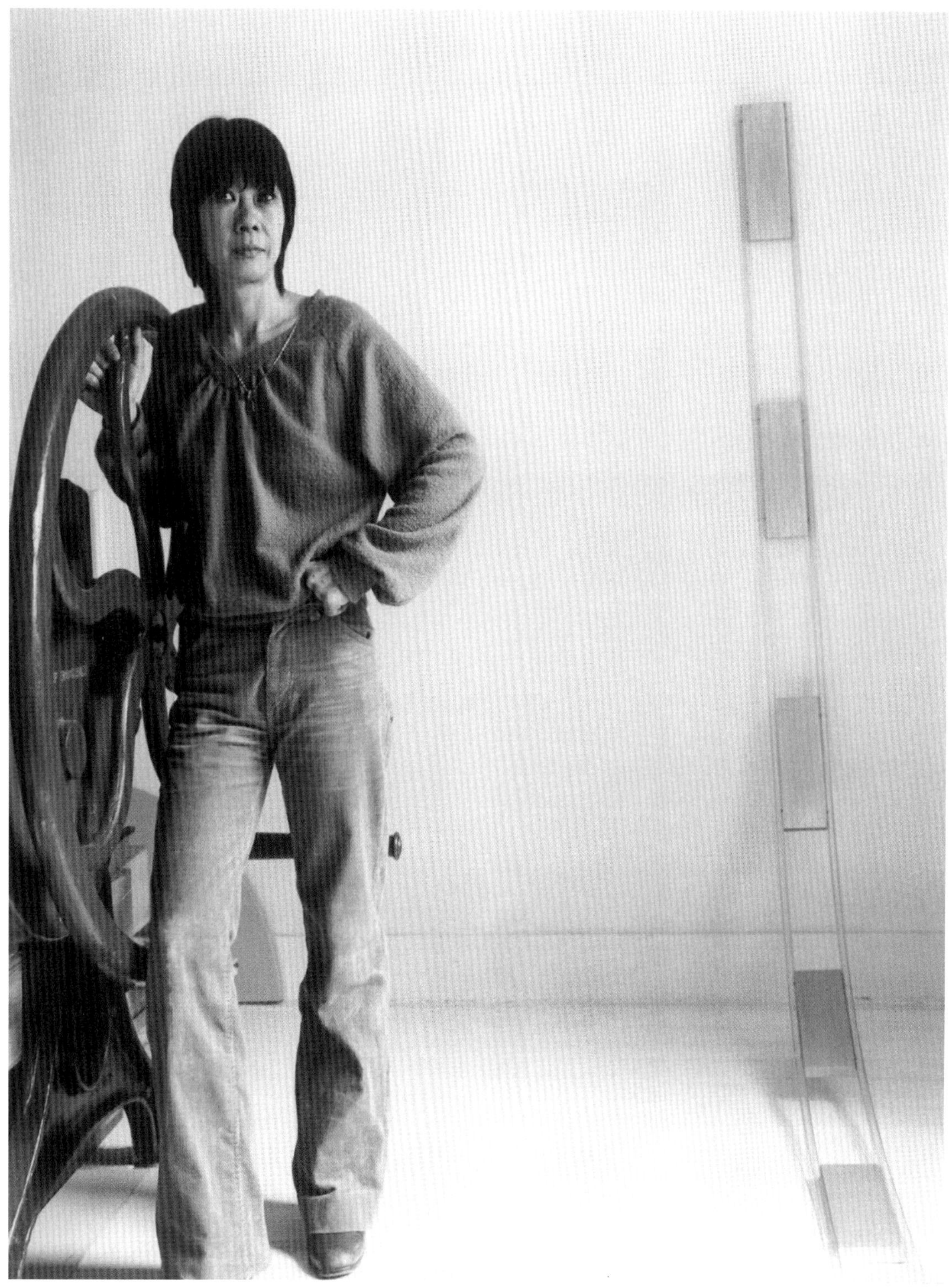

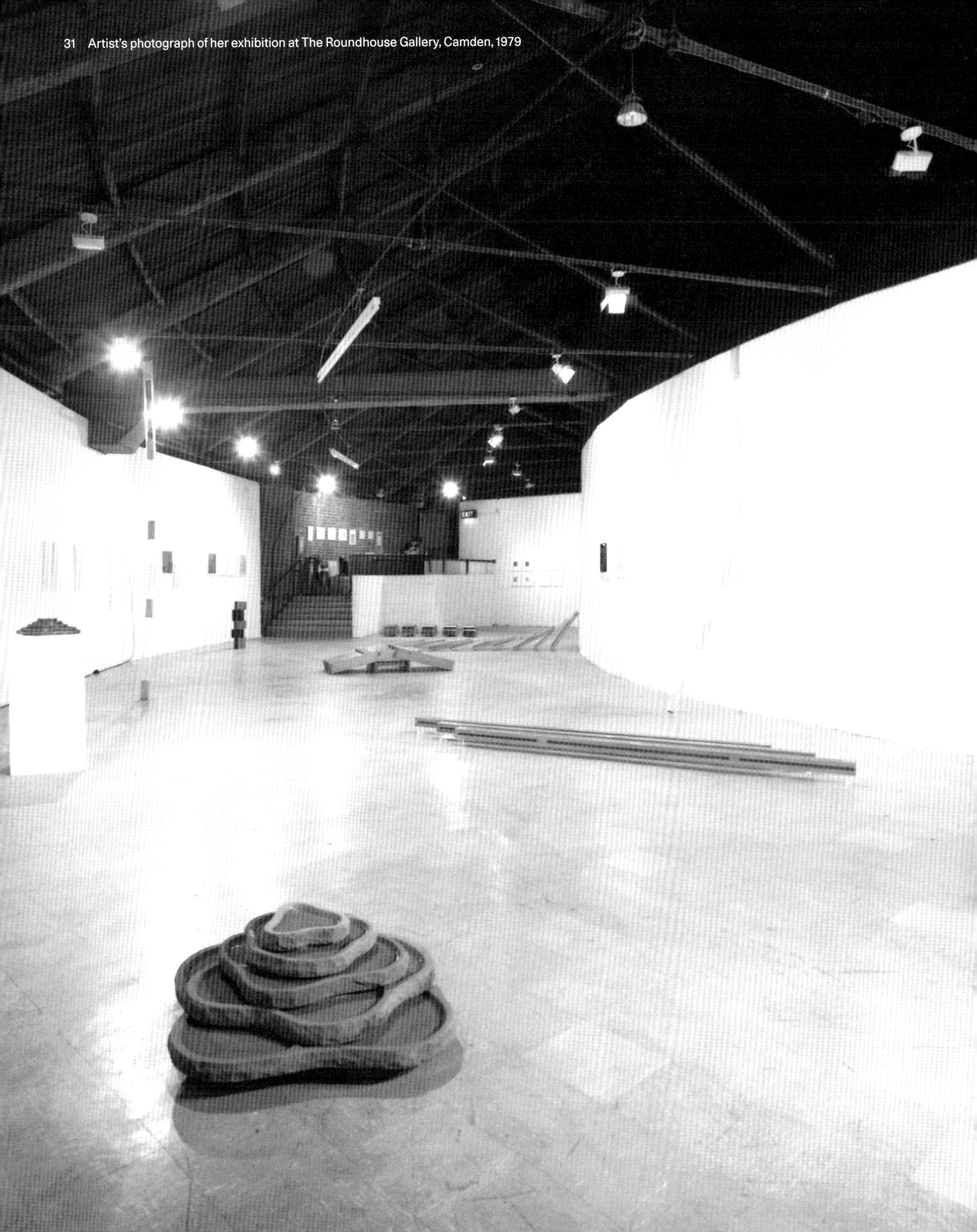

31 Artist's photograph of her exhibition at The Roundhouse Gallery, Camden, 1979

from a prescribed historical position. As some of the authors here indicate, Lim's unique and specific approaches both in her work and in her own understanding of her heritage can direct but not dictate the meaning we produce. As such, the qualities of space, rhythm and light that Lim saw as concerns in her sculpture are not just central themes in her practice, they are also symbolic lenses through which to explore the trajectory of her legacy and its contexts too. Just as Lim saw rhythms in the spaces between abstract forms activated by light, we too can look to the systemic gaps in our histories for ways to build inclusive forms of cultural knowledge. As Lim said herself, when beginning to use new materials, 'if you want to break the rules, you've first got to know what the rules are'.[23]

Notes

1 The portrait was a commission for the British Chinese Artists' Association.
2 Kim Lim, undated presentation notes, the Kim Lim archive.
3 Barbara Hepworth, quoted in Cindy Nemser, *Art Talk: Conversations with 12 Women Artists* (New York: Scribner, 1975), p.19.
4 See Joleen Loh, 'Relocating Kim Lim: A Cosmopolitan Perspective', *Southeast of Now*, vol.2, no.2 (October 2018), pp 33–62, and Joleen Loh, 'The Photographs of Kim Lim: A Visual Essay', *Art History*, vol.44 (2021), pp 532–52.
5 A further museum survey of Lim's work will be held at National Gallery Singapore in 2024, curated by Adele Tan and Joleen Loh.
6 *London, Asia* is a project led by Hammad Nasar and Sarah Victoria Turner and supported by the Paul Mellon Centre for Studies in British Art; https://www.paul-mellon-centre.ac.uk/research/london-asia.
7 https://www.arts.ac.uk/ual-decolonising-arts-institute/ual-related-activities/black-artists-and-modernism#:~:text=Black%20Artists%20and%20Modernism%20(BAM,in%20partnership%20with%20Middlesex%20University.
8 The sample was taken from 31 institutions which account for 1% of UK public art collections. With thanks to Dr Anjalie Dalal-Clayton, project researcher, who supplied these statistics to the author in April 2023.
9 See, for example, Sarah Victoria Turner and Jo Baring's podcast, *Sculpting Lives*, Season 1, Episode 3, released 7 April 2020.
10 Kim Lim, 'Breaking the Rules', *HOT* (1978), p.38.
11 Kim Lim, 'Statement', undated.
12 Kim Lim in notes written for Tate Gallery, London, 1977, unpaginated.
13 Julia Farrer, 'Kim Lim's Prints', *Kim Lim*, exhibition catalogue, SI2, p.74.
14 Kim Lim, quoted in Gene Baro, 'The Work of Kim Lim', *Studio International*, vol.176, no.905 (November 1968), p.186.
15 Kim Lim, Interview with Cathy Courtney, London, 20 October 1995, *National Life Stories: Artists' Lives* (London: British Library, 1995), C466/51, transcript, p.101.
16 Alex Turnbull, in *The Artist Speaks: Kim Lim* (Singapore: National Gallery Singapore, 2022), p.15.
17 Lucy Lippard, 'Introduction', *Hayward Annual 1978* (23 August–8 October 1978), exhibition catalogue published by the Arts Council, [n.p.].
18 Kim Lim, quoted in Sarah Kent, *Six Artists: Six Prints* (unpublished essay), p.3. Read by the author in the artist's archive.
19 Kim Lim, answering Lorna Green's survey in 1989, unpublished. The surveys are now held in the archives at The Hepworth Wakefield.
20 Kim Lim, quoted in Hetty Einzig, *Kim Lim*, exhibition catalogue, Nicola Jacobs Gallery, London, 1982, p.2.
21 Kim Lim, unpublished, undated interview with 'J.M.' as seen by the author in the artist's archives, 12 December 2022.
22 Lim, *Artists' Lives*, p.78.
23 Lim, 'Breaking the Rules', p.38.

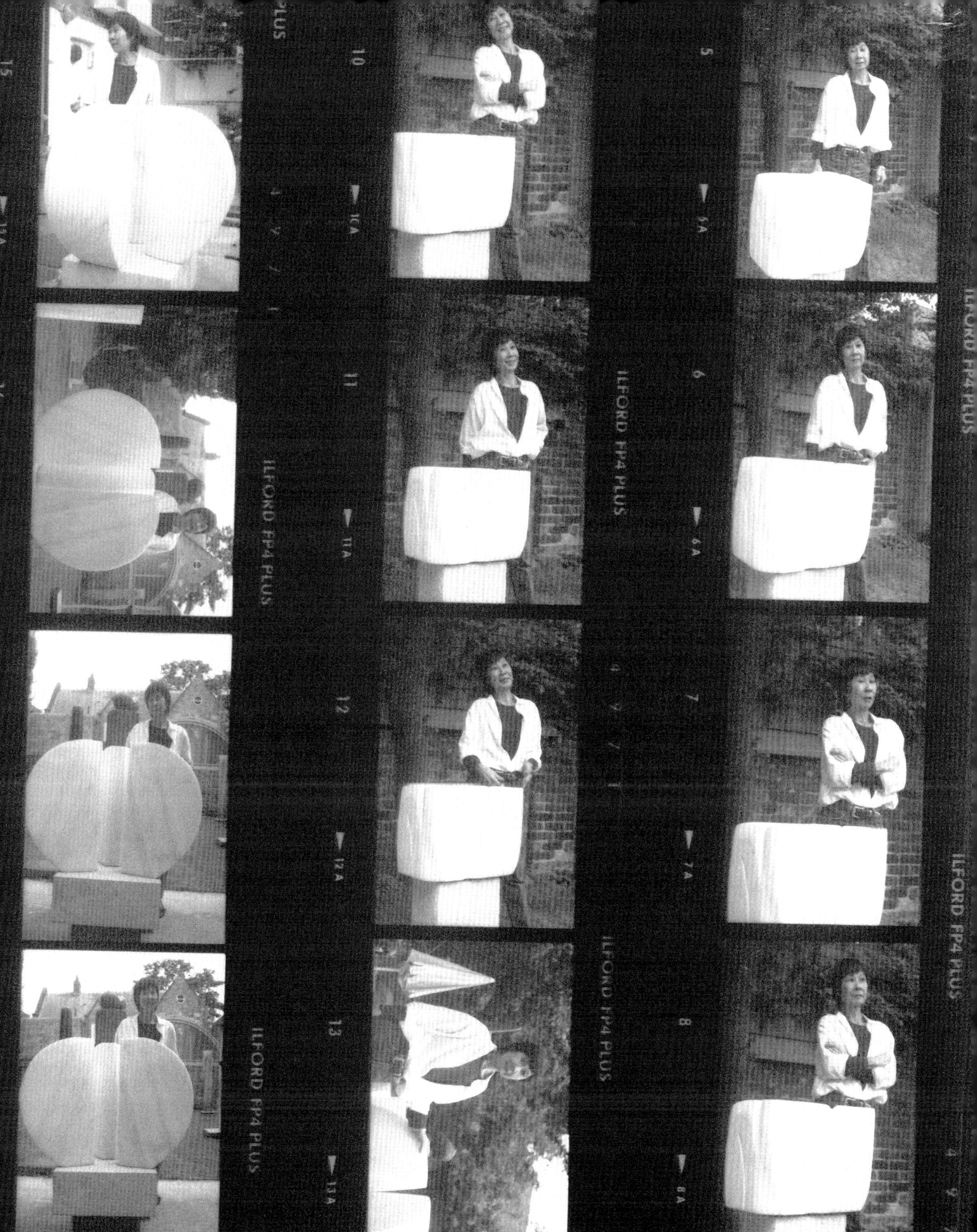

33 **Wind-Stone**, 1992 Portland stone, 140 × 20 × 70 cm (55 × 8 × 26 in) The Estate of Kim Lim

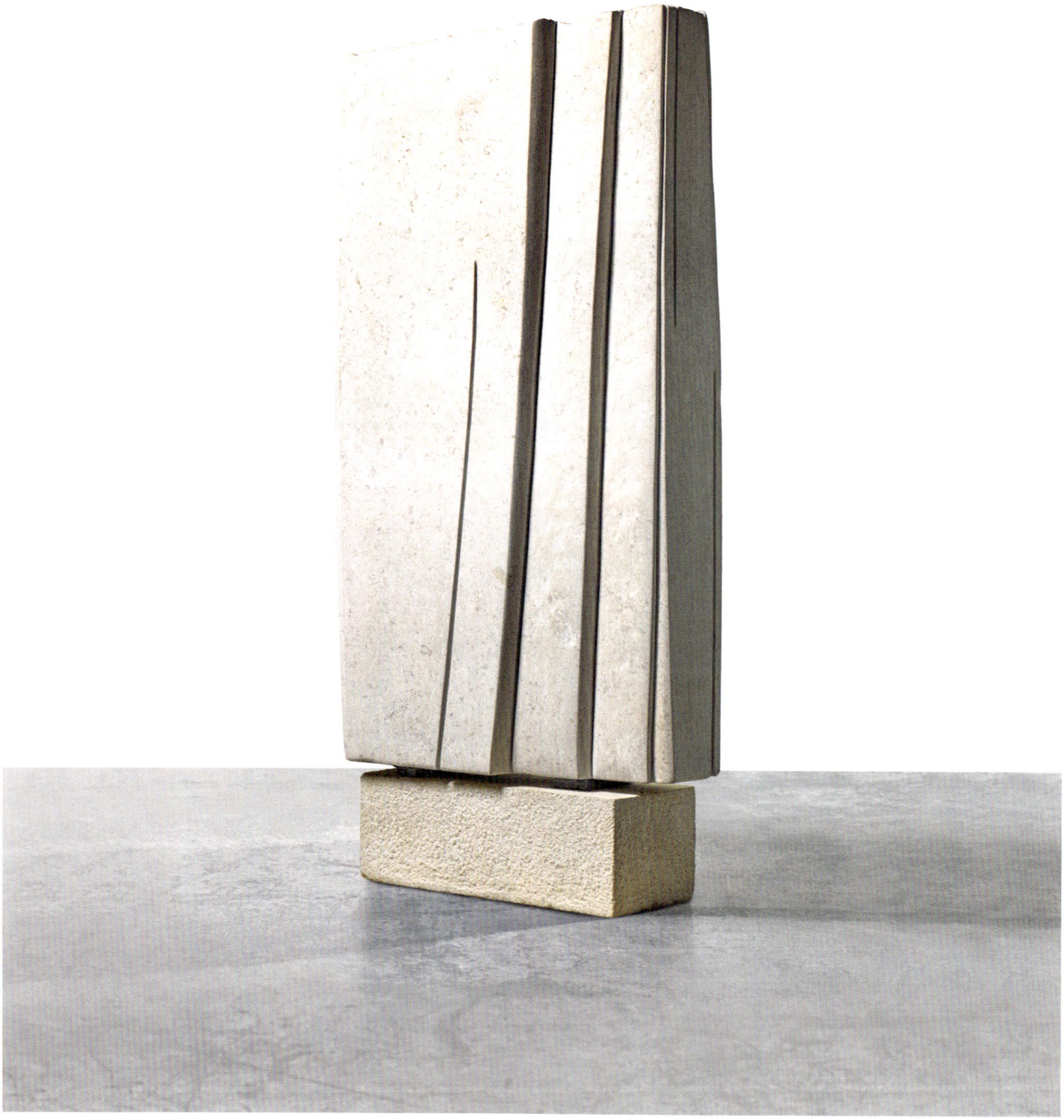

34 **Column**, 1984 Portland stone, 40 × 10·5 × 12·5 cm (16 × 4 × 5 in)
Private Collection

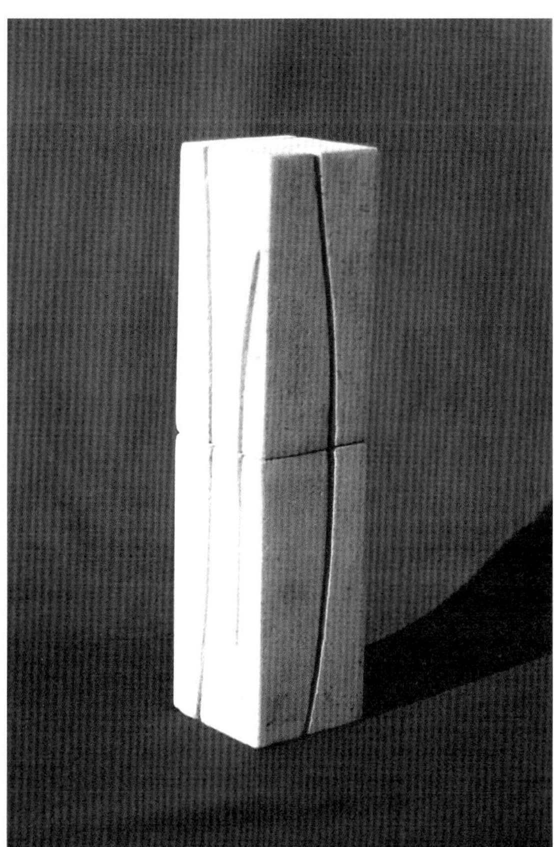

35 **Column P**, 1984 Portland stone, 97·5 × 20·3 × 20·5 cm (38 × 8 × 8 in)
Private Collection

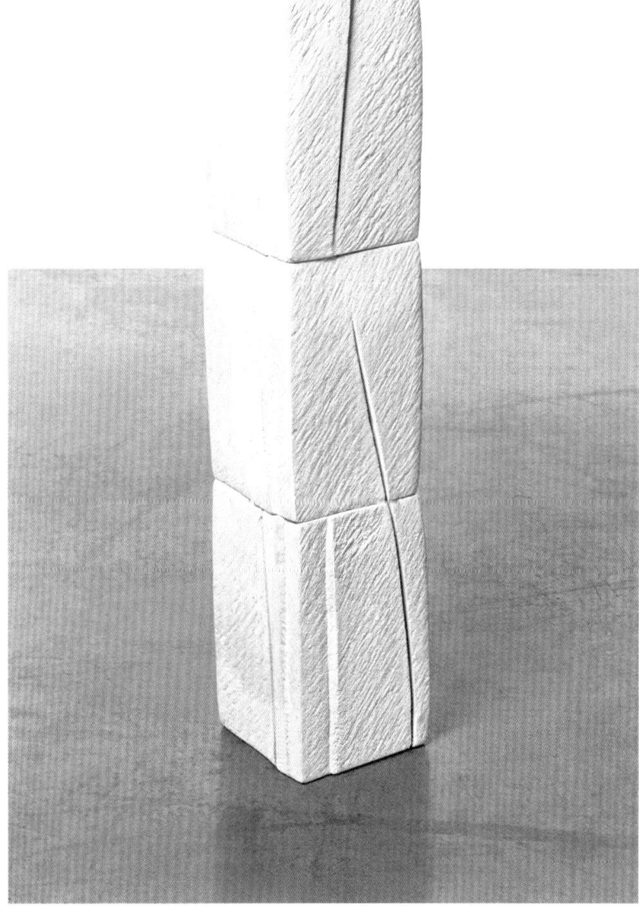

36 **III**, **IV**, **V**, 1993 lithographs on paper, 37 × 33·5 cm (15 × 13 in) The Estate of Kim Lim

37 **Untitled**, 1995 collage, 57 × 45 cm (22 × 8 in) The Estate of Kim Lim

38 **Kiss**, 1959 stone, dimensions not known The Estate of Kim Lim

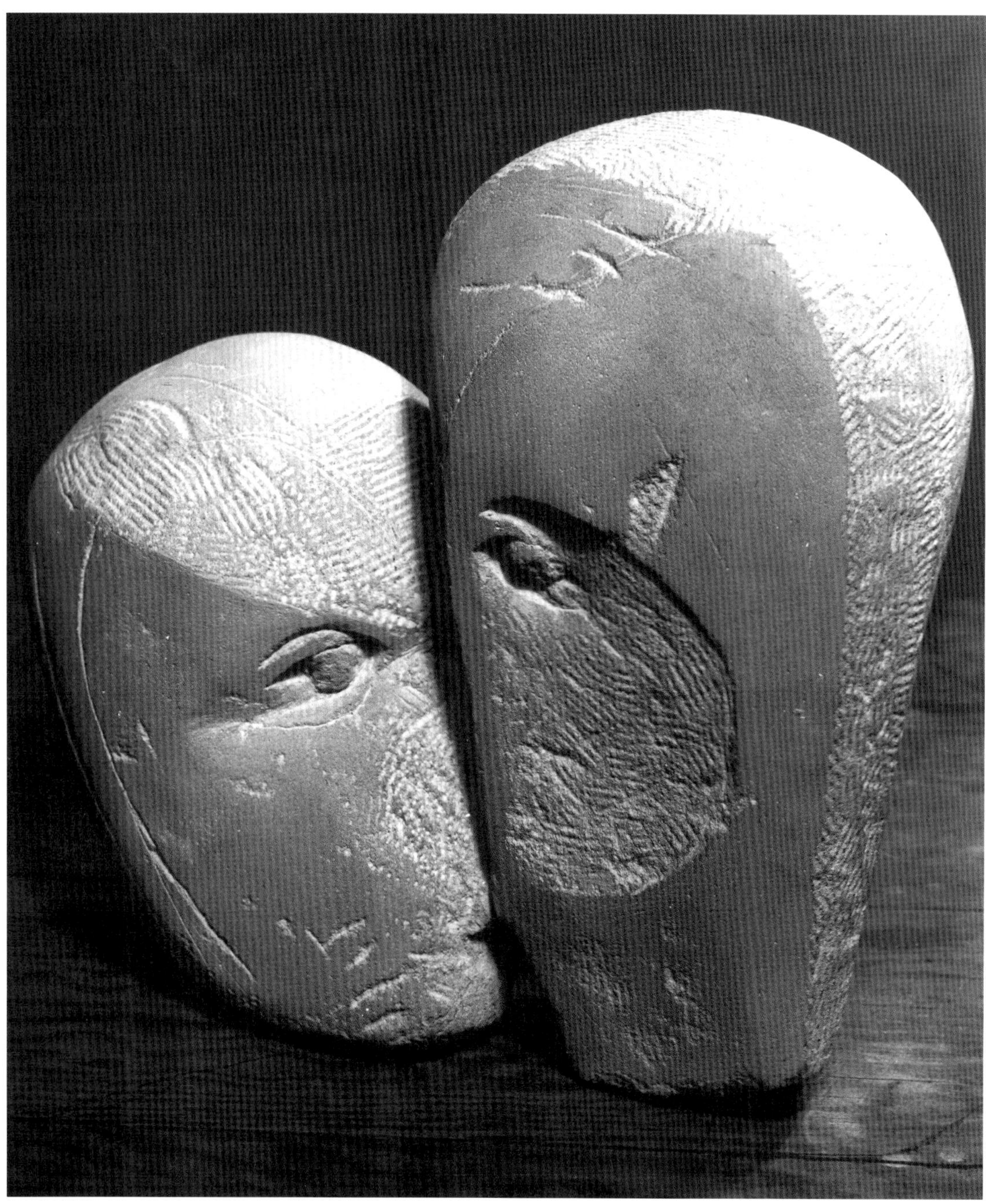

Ming Tiampo

'Space is the tension between forms': Contrapuntal Paradigms and Kim Lim's Essence of Form

> *What I am after is the activation of the spaces between, so that the space is the tension between forms.*
>
> – Kim Lim, 1968

In 1959 Kim Lim won second prize at the Slade School of Fine Art for the white marble sculpture *Kiss* (fig.38). Seemingly comprised of two separate pieces of stone, the work places them in tender relation with one another, carefully balanced in an embrace that both sustains and supports both beings. Although in dialogue with Brancusi's *Kiss* (1907–08), this work is very different in spirit and execution. While Brancusi's *Kiss* depicts two figures of almost equal size and shape, fused together as one block of stone in eternal embrace, Lim's *Kiss* eschews any negation of self. Each head is carved from a separate block of stone, and the two heads are of different sizes and shapes, one more rotund, the other elongated. The stones are carved as if suspended in a permanent state of approach. They only touch at a mid-point, the remainder of their faces separated by space and shadow. The eyes are locked together, but are placed at different levels on each head, suggesting two souls in charged erotic tension rather than one soul shared between two bodies, as in Brancusi's *Kiss.*

Kiss is emblematic of Lim's early practice while she was a student at the Slade, after leaving her course at St Martin's School of Art as can be seen in *Untitled* (1959; fig 40). It encapsulates a transition that she made in her work as she was moving out from Anthony Caro's sculpture studio at St Martin's, where he was still making figurative art, and towards a grammar of elemental form that grappled with fundamental questions of space, mass, edge and volume. In *Kiss* Lim manipulates the spaces between the heads to suggest forms in tension – perpetual movement, multiple lives and multiple worlds, arrested briefly by the magnetism of their connection. As her work moved away from figuration, this exploration of negative space as an element of tension between forms remained, both in her sculpture and in her graphic works. For example, her prints *Untitled* (1959–60; fig.41), *Red Split* (1960; fig.39)

39 **Red Split**, 1960 screenprint on paper, 39 × 58·5 cm (15 × 23 in) The Estate of Kim Lim

40 **Untitled**, 1959 materials and dimensions unknown The Estate of Kim Lim

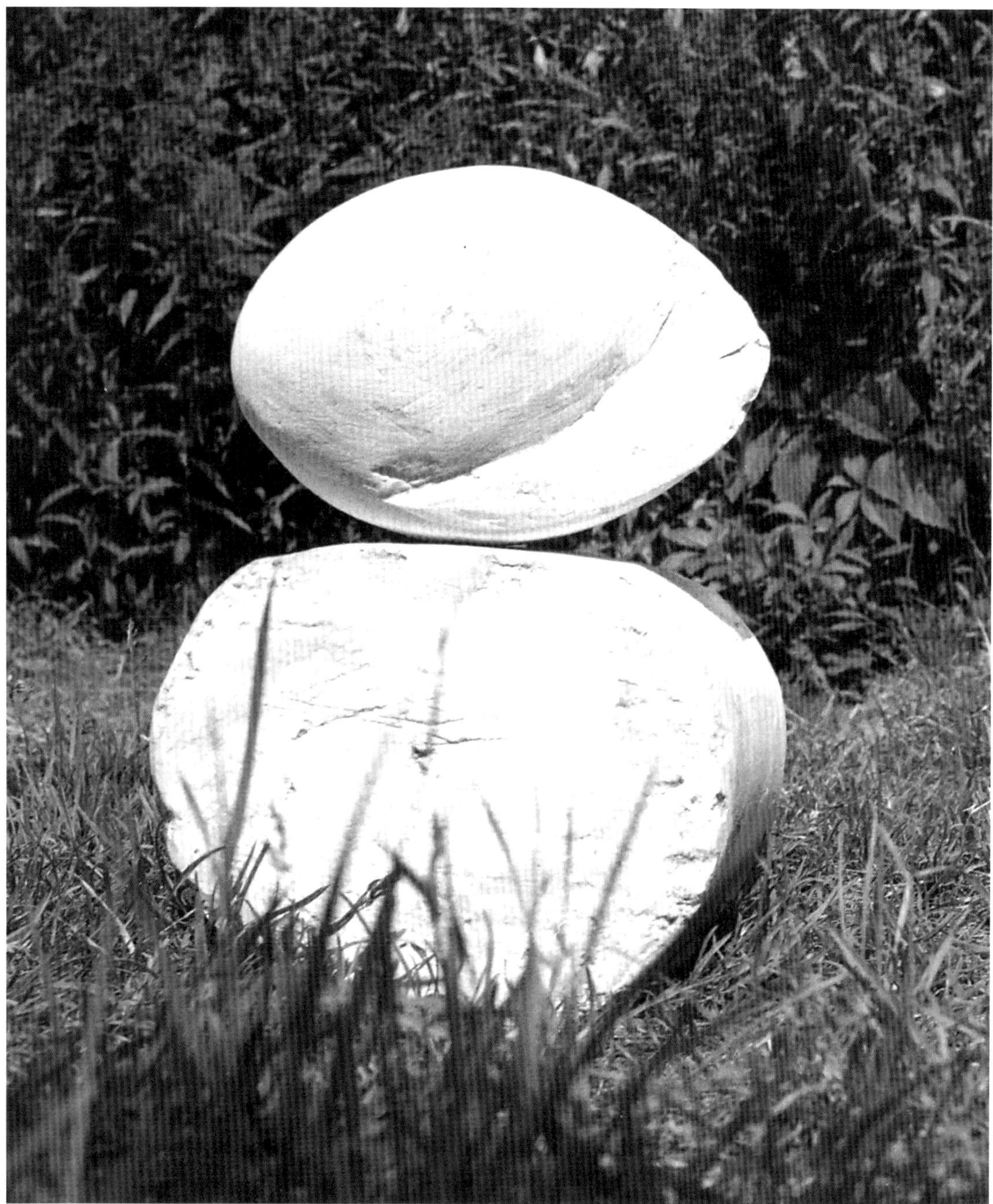

41 **Untitled**, 1959–60 lithograph on paper, 44·5 × 57·3 cm (18 × 22 in) The Estate of Kim Lim

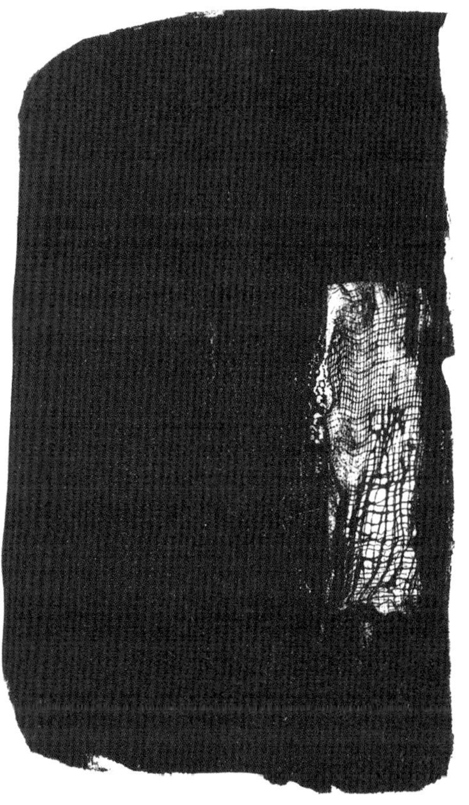

and *Head* (1960; fig.8) demonstrate a similar attention to the tension of in-between spaces, as do the sculptures *Narcissus* (1959; fig.12) and *King, Queen, Pawn* (1959; fig.7), and the screenprint of the same title made in 1960 (fig.6). In the 1970s Lim returned to address the question of negative space in her work, but with a different sensibility, employing it in serial, almost architectural modalities drawn from her explorations of Japanese and Chinese architectures as seen in her documentary photography (figs 42 and 43). This is evident in works such as *Ladder, Series 2* (1972; fig.44, *Gate* (1974), *Stack* (1975) and *Untitled* (1976; fig.45).

For Lim, the spaces in between were fundamental to her work, both as formal elements to be manipulated, and also as geographic and cultural spaces to be explored – Lim would travel extensively between Europe and Asia during her lifetime. Born in Singapore to a Peranakan Malay Straits Chinese family, Lim's cultural reference points were equally Chinese, Malay and English. Her father was a British-educated government magistrate – one of the first Chinese lawyers who had a degree that enabled him to enter the British colonial civil service – and was posted to Malacca, then Penang,

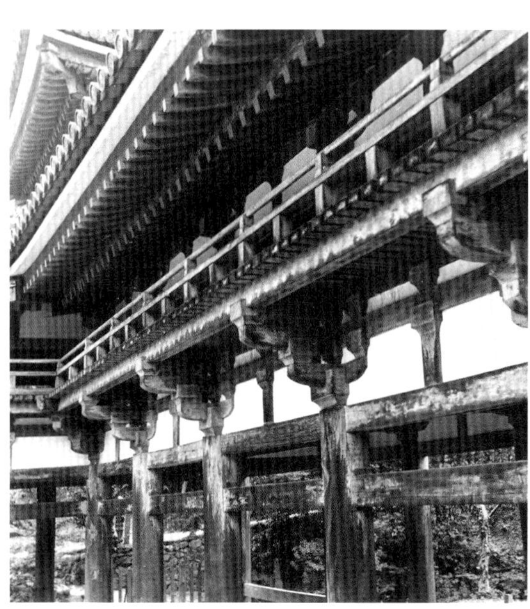

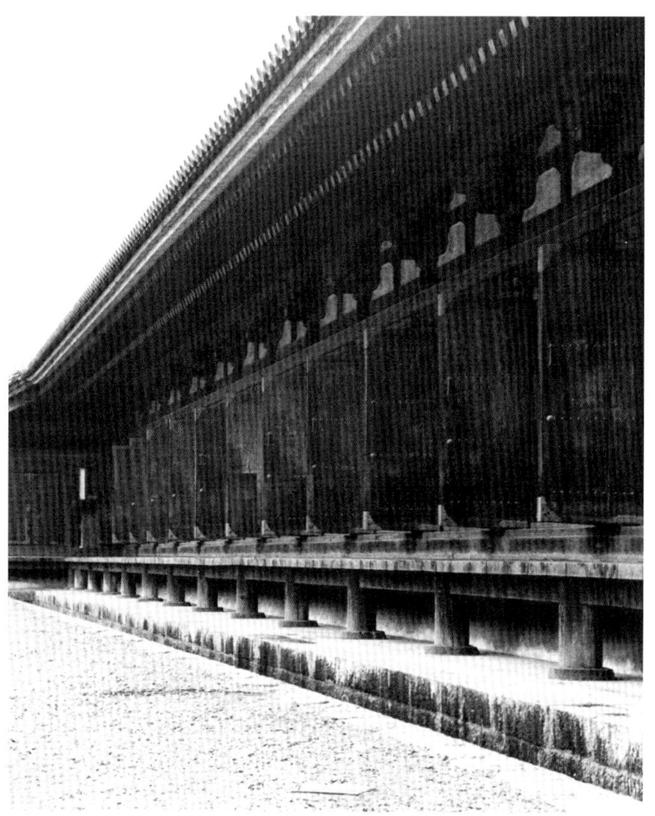

where the family spent the war under Japanese occupation. As a result of these overlapping histories of migration, colonisation and occupation, Lim's world was already highly transcultural before she moved to London in the autumn of 1954.

Lim began studying at St Martin's in 1954, before transferring to the Slade in 1957, graduating in 1960. At St Martin's she took general courses in drawing, sculpture and painting, following the Beaux Arts model of progressing from copying from plaster casts to nude models. She then specialised in sculpture, studying under Caro, but also learning to handle wood with a Basque artist she referred to as Joel Birdy.[1] Lim resisted Caro's figural practice, and the expectation that students would follow tradition. 'Struggling with figuration', as she put it, she was clearly unhappy, and was advised by sculptor Elisabeth Frink to move to the Slade.[2]

Although it too had its origins in the Beaux Arts model, the Slade School of Fine Art had been undergoing major changes since the appointment of William Coldstream in 1949. Under Coldstream, the curriculum was redesigned to promote methods of enquiry and observational practice, moving away from an idealised Beaux Arts progression, which naturalised Classical European figuration as the pinnacle of artistic achievement. The Slade thus provided a greater level of freedom to students wishing to define their own visual language. With an emphasis on rigour and an insistence on giving students the tools to situate themselves within larger discourses, Coldstream increased the focus on art-historical education at the Slade. As he wrote in his 1960 report of the National Advisory Council on Art Education, which introduced reforms to the entire UK art school system, 'The presence of art historians [has] enabled the student to understand relationships between his own activities and the culture within which he lives'.[3]

As for many other artists coming from the colonised and decolonising world, such as Lim's classmates Anwar Jalal Shemza from Pakistan (Slade, 1956–60) and Ibrahim El-Salahi from Sudan (Slade, 1954–7), the Art History classes at the Slade yielded mixed results for Lim. While the courses fulfilled Coldstream's goal of inviting students to critically situate their practices within a History of Art, the Eurocentrism of the curriculum left many artists from the Global Majority feeling marginalised at best and alienated at worst. In an often-repeated anecdote, for example, Shemza was sent into an artistic crisis after attending a lecture by Ernst Gombrich, the Slade art history lecturer. After hearing Gombrich dismiss all of Islamic art as 'functional', Shemza destroyed all of his previous work, 'everything that could be called "art"' and sought artistic solace in the Egyptian Wing of the British Museum.[4] Similarly, Lim bristled at the teleology of artistic achievement as European, commenting:

44 **Ladder Series 2**, 1972 etching on paper, 77 × 49·5 cm (30 × 19 in) The Estate of Kim Lim

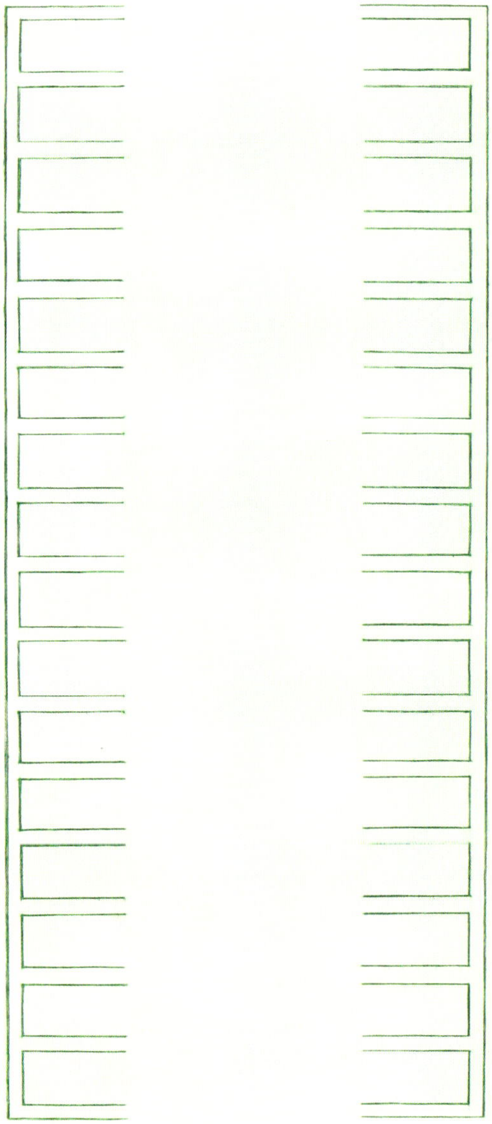

45 **Untitled**, 1976 paper, 45 × 47 cm (18 × 19 in) The Estate of Kim Lim

> when I went to the Slade there was Art History where you learnt that … there [was] primitive art … leading up to the kind of epitome of Western art, which is the Renaissance, and I still don't feel that way … there were other things equally good … I mean the first time I saw Michelangelo I thought wow! Fantastic, but he didn't really move me; he impressed me. So in the end, you just have to go according to your instincts.[5]

Accustomed to negotiating between cultural spaces and between British and Japanese colonial masters, Lim 'followed her instincts' and took her education into her own hands. She resisted both the Eurocentric narratives that she was being given *and* essentialist suggestions from professors and interlocutors that she situate her work within Chinese art. Instead, she literally explored the geographic, cultural, artistic, historic and temporal spaces *between* London and Singapore. In the summers between academic years, Lim took advantage of the half-fare student tickets that allowed her to stop at any point between the two cities. During these trips, which she characterised as her 'main art education',[6] she travelled voraciously, visiting museums and monuments wherever she could. Lim recounted she

> would take a plane and stop off, not knowing anybody in a place, and spend a couple of days there … and then go around looking at museums. And I saw, I stopped off at India and went to see Aurangabad and, you know, and Ellora, and that was a great revelation for me, to see things in its place where it was meant to be, in the light that it was meant to be … I was like a sponge in those days, didn't know anything, so everything was just amazing and marvellous, and going to Ellora where these temples were carved out of solid rock, and these huge figures, you know. It was just thrilling.[7]

Lim's study trips took her to Italy, Egypt, Cambodia, India, Japan and other places, enabling her to develop a visual vocabulary that Joleen Loh describes as proposing 'multiple spatio-temporal coordinates for sculpture – that is, the complex historical precedents for her sculpture in many cultures across time, beyond the telos of western art history'.[8] Loh argues that the pinboards of photographs that Lim took on her travels served as studies for her work, 'wherein her interests in the interaction between space, light, and object were explored using a photographic syntax'.[9] In other words, as we can see through her photographs of the Kiyomizu-dera temple (fig.46), which consider how space, grid and structure operate, Lim's travels were not just an artistic education, but artistic research. Indeed, Lim described the relationships between artistic traditions as follows:

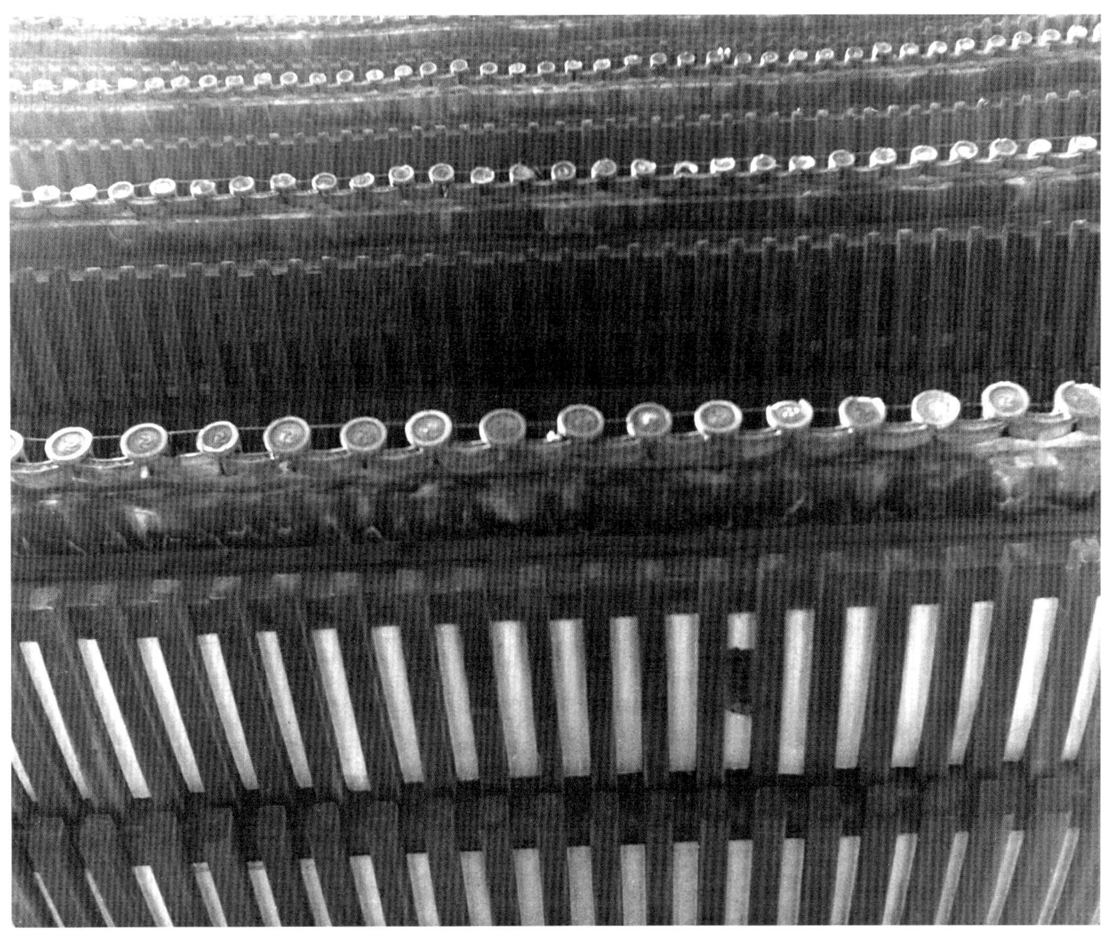

46 Kim Lim, Kiyomizu-dera temple, Kyoto, Japan, *c.*1962 The Estate of Kim Lim

> Sculpture of all times and societies deal[s] ... with many of the same basic issues and shared attitudes, or declares quite opposite positions about such matters as the relationship of space and mass. The obvious differences, subject matter, and superficial treatment, often hide important similarities and sympathies. For me, the experience of sculpture, West and East, taught me what sculpture is about. Experience gave me the motive to go on.[10]

The key term that Lim uses here is *experience*, an embodied encounter with sculpture rather than a purification of abstract form, distinguishing her approach from the universalism of American and British Minimalism. In fact, she even stated quite boldly that 'truth to material has never been very much my concern'.[11] Rather, Lim's approach is *contrapuntal*,[12] putting into relation multiple melodic lines and creating work that entangles her literal journey between metropole and colony with its imbricated histories, aesthetics, epistemologies and temporalities. These explorations of the spaces in between are at times made visible through her use of titles, like whitecaps that reveal the presence of wave energy in the ocean. While *Ronin* (1963; fig.18) plays on the notion of the wandering samurai without a master as a metaphor for the mobilities of modernisms, *Trengannu II* (1968; fig.79) refers to a state in Malaysia where Lim experienced the sublime beauty of watching sea turtles lay eggs on the beach, perhaps even understanding the turtles' 'ever-winding circles' as they close up their nests as a kind of non-human sculptural form.[13]

By using a combination of deep research, allusive titles and analytic form, Lim (in her words) 'simplifies the image, realizes it in terms of *essential features.* I don't mean minimalises or reduces it.'[14] This distinction is a crucial one, in that it reveals the complex paradigms enacted by Lim's works: the creation of new coordinates for understanding sculpture, and a contrapuntal exploration of the essence of form.

Notes

1 Kim Lim refers to 'the Basque teacher Joel Birdy' in an oral interview, but the transcription notes that a phonetic spelling was supplied. See Kim Lim, Interview with Cathy Courtney, London, 20 October 1995, *National Life Stories: Artists' Lives* (London: British Library, 1995), C466/51, transcript p.93.
2 Lim, ibid., p.97.
3 Ministry of Education, First Report of the National Advisory Council on Art Education (London: Her Majesty's Stationery Office, 1960), p.11.
4 Anwar Jalal Shemza, *A.J. Shemza: Paintings Drawings 1957–1963*, exhibition catalogue (Durham: Gulbenkian Museum of Oriental Art and Archaeology, 1963), p.4.
5 Lim, *Artists' Lives*, pp 95–6.
6 ibid., p.97.
7 ibid., p.95.
8 Joleen Loh, 'Relocating Kim Lim: A Cosmopolitan Perspective', *Southeast of Now: Directions in Contemporary and Modern Art in Asia* 2, no.2 (October 2018), p.44.
9 ibid., p.41.
10 Quoted in Gene Baro, 'The Work of Kim Lim', *Studio International*, vol.176, no.905 (November 1968), p.187.
11 ibid., p.188.
12 See Edward W. Said, *Culture and Imperialism* (New York: Vintage, 1993), p.51.
13 Lim, *Artists' Lives*, p.70.
14 Quoted in Baro, 'The Work of Kim Lim', p.188.

47 Kim Lim *c*.1980 The Estate of Kim Lim

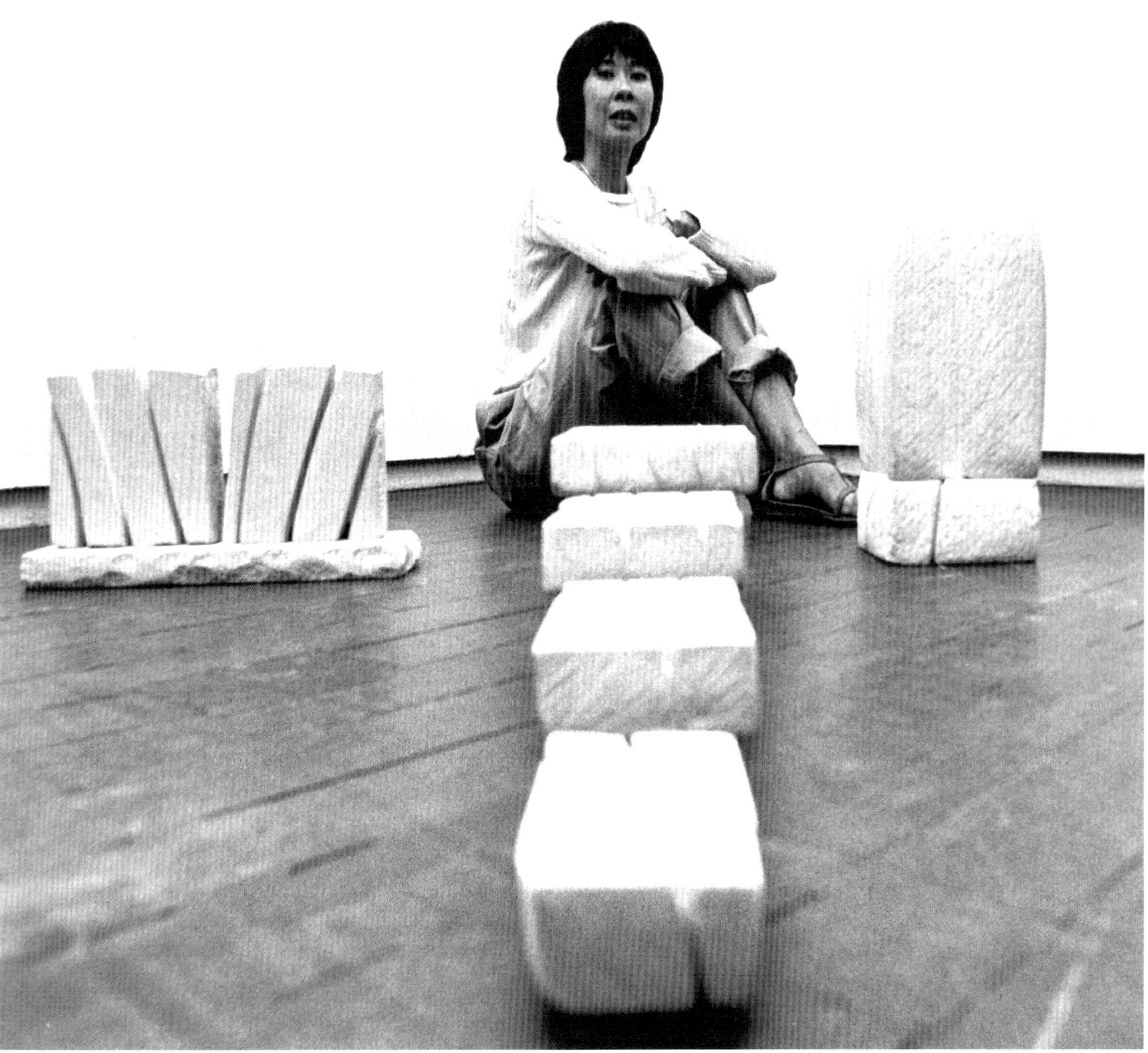

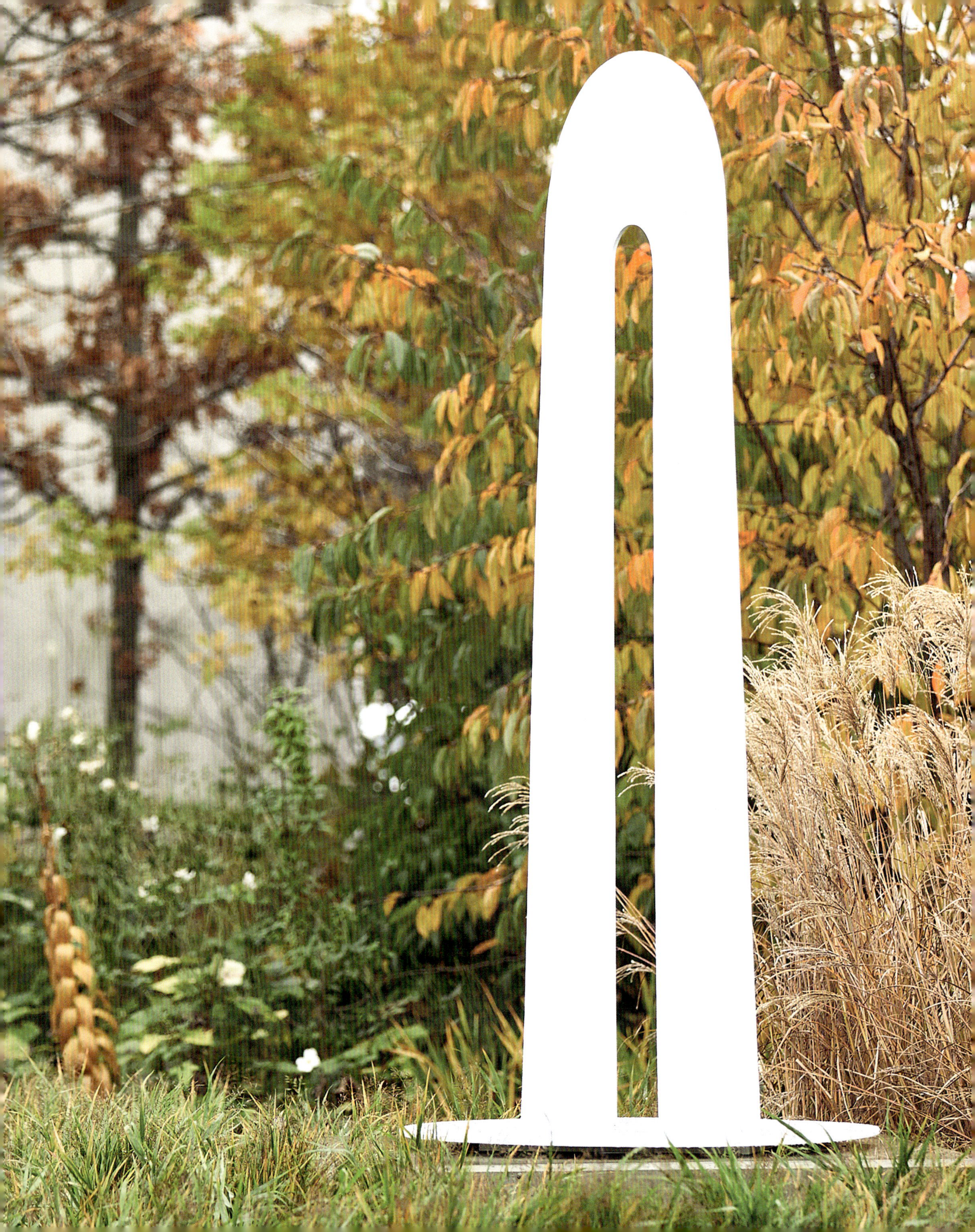

Wenny Teo

The Light of Day

'My interest is to give the experience of more than is there', said Kim Lim in an interview with *Studio International* in 1968, alluding to an important conceptual reorientation in her practice.[1] While her earlier wooden sculptures had gravitated towards problems of edge, mass, density and volume, by the mid-1960s Lim had begun to experiment with different materials and scales to evoke more subtle, phenomenological effects. To draw out these elusive properties most efficiently, she continued: 'It's important for me ... to make a clear, unfussy statement of form. The form is literally there; there is no illusionism or other trickery in stating it. I want the form to be essential to the effect of more from less, but the form itself must be self-sufficient, sculpturally pertinent – apt.'[2]

The artist then cited the example of *Day* (1966; fig.48), a work she had made two years earlier as the 'clearest image' of how these formal dynamics play out in her work. *Day* is a striking outdoor sculpture that was presented to the collection of Wakefield Art Gallery Collection in 1983, and now stands in the landscaped curtilage of The Hepworth Wakefield Garden.[3] Rising to a height of 2.15 metres from a simple disc at the base, it is comprised of a thick ribbon of sand-blasted steel, curved at the apex to form a narrow elliptical archway. It is one of Lim's largest sculptures as well as her most monumental in its arresting frontality. As one moves to view it from the side, however, the entire structure seems to collapse before our eyes into a mere sliver, fully disclosing the flatness of its industrial make and materiality. Even when seen from the front, there is a sense of lightness and transparency to the work, accentuated by its highly reflective surface, which had first been primed with a layer of zinc for added protection against weathering, and finished with a smooth layer of white enamel 'yacht' paint. As Lim emphasised in a letter to the gallery discussing its future maintenance, 'The sculpture should look luminous'.[4]

Depending on its orientation and location, the polished surface of the work becomes a screen for the ambient flux of wider meteorological and seasonal conditions: when sited in open space and seen in direct sunlight, it appears to glow like a beacon; and when placed in a more shaded area, veiled by a flickering patina of arboreal shadows, it almost disappears into the background. As its title suggests, *Day* also functions as a rudimentary gnomon of sorts – the raised part of the sundial that casts a shadow – indexically registering the

48 **Day**, 1966 painted steel,
215 × 96·3 × 2 cm (85 × 38 × 1 in)
Wakefield Council Permanent Art Collection
(The Hepworth Wakefield)

passage of time by mapping the wider cosmic, diurnal and circadian rotations and rhythms of the earth onto the sculpture's immediate surrounds.

In this, *Day* marked an important turning point in Lim's sculptural practice – foreshadowing the dynamic interplay of form, light, space and rhythm that would come to characterise her celebrated later work in the 1980s. Nevertheless, it is a piece that sits somewhat awkwardly in Lim's oeuvre. Its smooth, industrially fabricated steel surface is quite unlike the hand-crafted, rough-hewn textures of the wood and stone sculptures that preceded and followed her work in this period. Although Lim produced other steel sculptures, *Day* stands out among them for its verticality and symmetry. What is of interest here is also the very precise terminology that Lim used to describe the work: the insistence on making a clear 'statement of form', that is 'self-sufficient', 'literally there' and 'apt', without 'illusionism' or 'trickery'. Her reference to these terms indicates a critical engagement with the fraught artistic debates in Britain and America at the time, between artists and critics who sought to uphold the modernist tenets of medium-specificity, purity and presence against the 'literalness', 'objecthood' and 'theatricality' that was seen to characterise the work of a new generation of Minimalist artists.[5] Looking more closely at the context in which *Day* was first exhibited sheds light on how Lim sought to position her practice within and against these wider art-historical trajectories, discourses and movements.

Day was made at a pivotal moment in Lim's career. A few months before her first ever solo exhibition, held at the Axiom Gallery in 1966, it was first exhibited at *Sculpture in the Open Air* at Battersea Park – a triennial series of outdoor displays organised by London City Council between 1948 and the mid-1970s, intended to introduce the wider public to modern British sculpture in a leisurely, parkland environment.[6] The 1966 edition was the first 'all-British' exhibition and included luminaries such as Barbara Hepworth and Henry Moore alongside the 'New Generation' of sculptors, represented by Phillip King, David Annesley, Michael Bolus, William Tucker, Lim's partner William Turnbull and her former tutor at St Martin's, Anthony Caro. For the curator Alan Bowness, the selection attested to how 'we are witnessing in this country, here and now, one of the greatest epochs in the history of art'.[7]

The fact that a Singapore-born woman artist was included in this display of epoch-defining British art, in this most English of settings no less, was a rather remarkable achievement – especially since, at the age of 30, Lim was also one of the youngest participants. On formal grounds at least, *Day* was an obvious choice. As Bowness observed in his catalogue essay, one of the defining features of contemporary sculpture of the time was the use of modern technological materials like welded steel to completely rethink 'the function of space'.[8]

Caro is often regarded as a pioneer in the use of steel, and he had no fewer than three works included in the exhibition, each representative of the spatial dynamics that Bowness was referring to: highly asymmetrical, welded steel constructions that lay close to the ground, characterised by a fragmented horizontality that was deliberately not monolithic or monumental. Caro's constructions 'invade space in a complicated way', making 'full visual assimilation of the work difficult.' [9]

Although *Day* is similarly fabricated from painted steel, its stakes are clearly other. Unlike the volatile geometry of Caro's sculptures in the exhibition, *Day* is streamlined, rounded and symmetrical. Lim would later refer to the sculpture as a 'single entity' that should be 'perceived all at once', so that the process of walking around it would add to the experience, 'confirming what [the viewer] has understood of it'. [10] In this, the work generates a spatial encounter that is less invasive and disorienting than it is immediate and expansive. Lim often wrote of the sense of wonder conferred by the archaic structures she visited on her travels between Europe and Asia. Standing between the pillars of the Acropolis in Athens, she recalled, 'gives you such a sensation of space, inside/outside, of place, of magic of scale', while in Japan she encountered 'structures [that] can be opened to let nature in ... those freestanding "gates" that give you such a specific feeling of entering although all you have around you is open space'. [11] *Day* certainly speaks to how a singular form can evoke sensations of boundlessness – amplifying the changing environment that surrounds it, and casting the immaterial contingencies of space, time and light into sharp relief.

Such a 'clear, unfussy statement of form' is testament to how Lim sought to carve out an independent position vis-à-vis the artistic conventions of the time, signalling her awareness of and engagement with prevailing art-historical discourse and debates, but also a critical distance and difference from them. She absorbed and adapted various stylistic and perceptual modalities from often contrasting schools of thought and redeployed them on her own terms. In this, it is possible to consider the exacting importance she placed on 'self-sufficient' form in the light of her perceived 'otherness' as well.

Although Lim continued to enjoy considerable success in her lifetime, particularly in the UK, her achievements were often eclipsed by the fact that she was, as she acknowledged, 'female and foreign' – and at times they were overshadowed by those of her husband, William Turnbull. In a short article in the Scottish *Daily Mail* profiling Lim and the Battersea Park exhibition, the writer dismissively referred to *Day* as an 'adipose croquet hoop', made by an artist 'who is married to one of Britain's well-known sculptors'. [12] In 1977 Lim was the only woman artist to be included in the first Hayward Annual and was subsequently one of five women artists on the jury of the 1978 edition –

a panel assembled following the lack of women in the first exhibition in 1975 (fig.51). Lim's involvement came under fire due to her association with Turnbull, who had been one of the jurors of the 1977 exhibition.[13] In 1988 Lim decided not to participate in Rasheed Araeen's seminal exhibition *The Other Story: Afro-Asian Artists in Post-war Britain*, again at the Hayward, in 1989, explaining in a letter to the curator that she did not want to 'other herself'.[14] She later clarified, 'what was important in the end was what I did, not where I came from. Race and gender were "givens" I work from – perhaps the work does reflect this – but I did not want to make them an issue.'[15]

As Kobena Mercer has pointed out, all too often critical assessments of the work of ethnic 'minority' artists tend to be grounded in their biography and personal geography in a way that 'overshadows, if not completely obliterates ... the aesthetic work performed by the object itself'.[16] Or as Joan Kee wryly put it, 'why invest real thought into the problem of form when everyone just wants to know where you're from?'[17] Lim was an artist who continued to 'invest real thought' in the problem of form throughout her lifetime, continually recalibrating and reorienting her practice to address certain material and experiential concerns.

Lim admitted that the 'the sense of not "belonging" felt a little isolating at times but it had the compensating element of freedom – a certain feeling of detachment from which one could view both East and West'.[18] This critical distance was manifest in her refusal to be dragged into the orbit of circuitous art-historical discourses and the politics of otherness and exclusion they often engender; but this is not to say that her work and its critical reception does not register the push and pull of these wider systems and structures.

In her book *Forms: Whole, Rhythm, Hierarchy, Network* the literary theorist Caroline Levine wrote, 'Rather than asking what artists intend or even what forms *do*, we can ask instead what potentialities lie latent – though not always obvious – in aesthetic and social arrangements'.[19] Levine borrows the term 'affordances' from design theory to describe how certain materials and objects connote specific functions and actions. 'Affordances point us to both what all forms are capable of – to the range of uses each could be put to ... but also to their limits, the restrictions intrinsic to particular materials and organising principles.'[20] A crucial vector of Lim's work, already established in the 'apt' form of *Day*, is how it mobilises the viewer in the encounter, causing us to continually reorientate ourselves in relation to it, to see the work from different angles and in different light. We might think of the work as what Sarah Ahmed called an 'orientation device', that makes us aware of the 'different ways of registering the proximity of objects and others', as 'orientations shape not only how we inhabit space, but how we apprehend this world of shared inhabitance, as well as "who" or "what" we direct our energy and attention towards'.[21]

Notes

1 Kim Lim, quoted in Gene Baro, 'The Work of Kim Lim', *Studio International*, vol.176, no.905 (November 1968), p.188.
2 ibid.
3 There is a second version of *Day* also made in 1966 held in the collection of National Gallery Singapore.
4 Lim, in an undated letter to Corrine Miller, Keeper of Art, Wakefield Art Gallery, 19 March 1983, the archives of The Hepworth Wakefield.
5 These debates are effectively summarised in James Meyer, *Art and Polemics in the Sixties* (New Haven: Yale University Press, 2001). Robert Morris's influential 'Notes on Sculpture' was published in *Artforum* in February 1966, and interestingly William Turnbull (Lim's husband) published an article of the same name in the same issue of *Studio International* as Lim's interview with Gene Baro (see note 1).
6 See Jennifer Powell, 'A coherent, national "school" of sculpture? Constructing post-war New British Sculpture through exhibition practices', *Sculpture Journal*, vol.21, no.2 (2012), pp 37–50.
7 Alan Bowness, 'Introduction', in *Sculpture in the Open Air: An exhibition of contemporary British sculpture in Battersea Park*', May–September 1966, exhibition catalogue (London: GLC Parks Department, 1966), unpaginated.
8 ibid.
9 William Rubin, *Anthony Caro*, exhibition catalogue (New York: Museum of Modern Art, 1975), p.66.
10 Kim Lim, unpublished writings, the Kim Lim archive. Lim also emphasised that the work should be seen in its 'entirety' in a short video segment from the documentary series *Look at Life*, that profiled the Battersea exhibition. 'Things in Space', *Look at Life*, 1966, Rank Organisation.
11 Lim, unpublished writings, the Kim Lim archive.
12 Arthur Richards, 'S'pore girl now a sculptress in London', *Sunday Mail* (3 July 1966), p.6.
13 'What the critics said', *Art Monthly* (1 June 1977), p.8.
14 Kim Lim, letter to Andrew Dempsey, 9 June 1988. Rasheed Araeen Archives at Art Asia Archive, Hong Kong. Araeen expressed his 'particular sadness' at not having Lim in the exhibition, as 'her absence has left a big gap in the Story, because she was both an important modern sculptor in the 60s and after, and a *woman* artist who has not received due recognition'. Rasheed Araeen, 'Postscript', in *The Other Story: Afro-Asian Artists in Post-war Britain* (London: Hayward Gallery, Southbank Centre, 1989), p.106.
15 Lim, unpublished writings, the Kim Lim archive.
16 Kobena Mercer, 'Iconography after Identity', in David A. Bailey, Ian Baucom and Sonia Boyce (eds), *Shades of Black: Assembling Black Arts in 1980s Britain* (Durham, NC: Duke University Press, 2005), pp 52–3.
17 Joan Kee, 'Form in service of the global', in Alexander Dumbadze and Suzanne Hudson (eds), *Contemporary Art: 1989 to the Present* (Oxford: Wiley Blackwell, 2013), p.98.
18 Lim, unpublished writings.
19 Caroline Levine, *Forms: Whole, Rhythm, Hierarchy, Network* (Princeton, NJ: Princeton University Press, 2015), p.6.
20 ibid., p.10.
21 Sarah Ahmed, *Queer Phenomenology: Orientations, Objects, Others* (Durham, NC: Duke University Press, 2006), p.3.

Overleaf: 49 Kim Lim's studio *c.*2012, Camden Square, London, no date
The Estate of Kim Lim

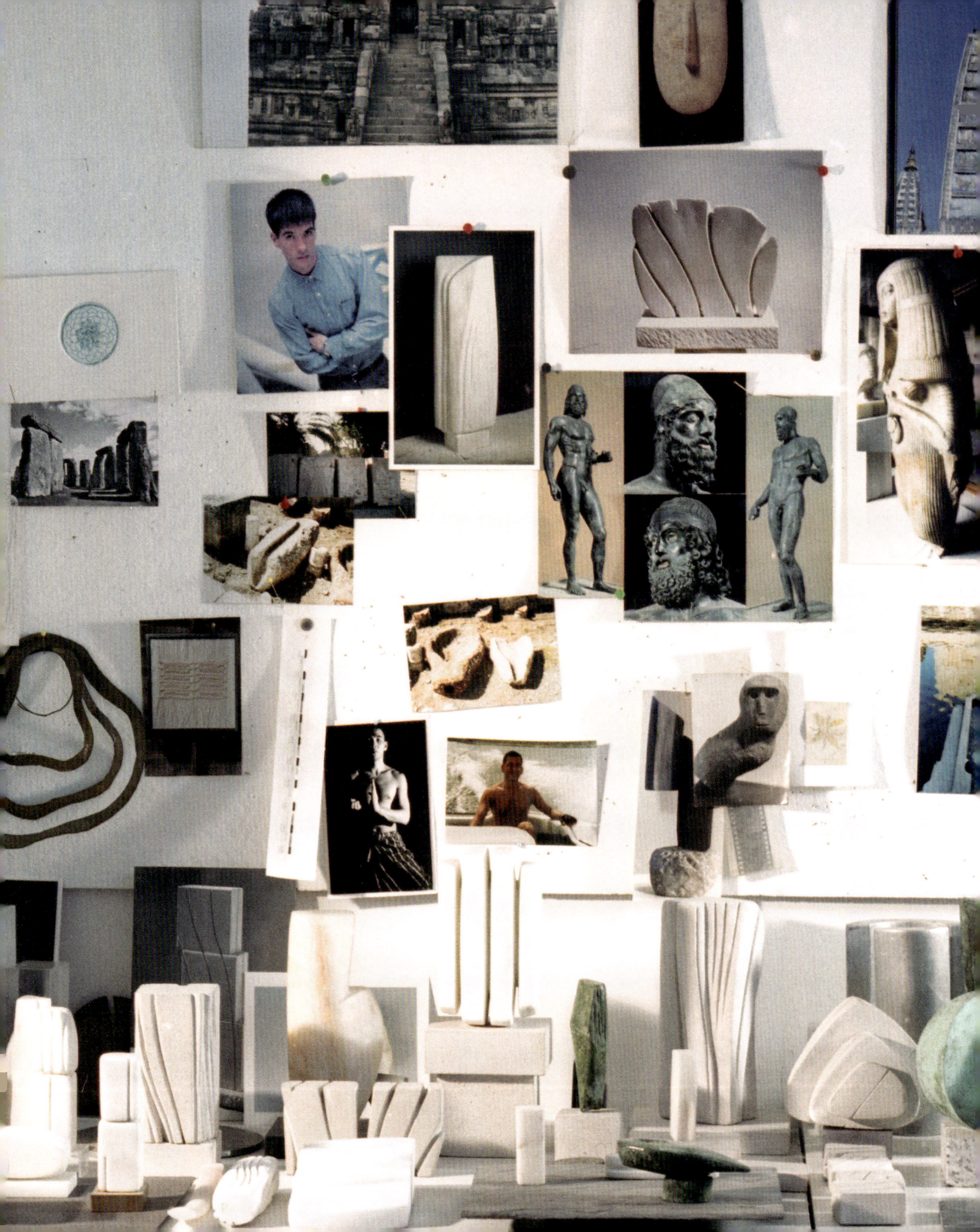

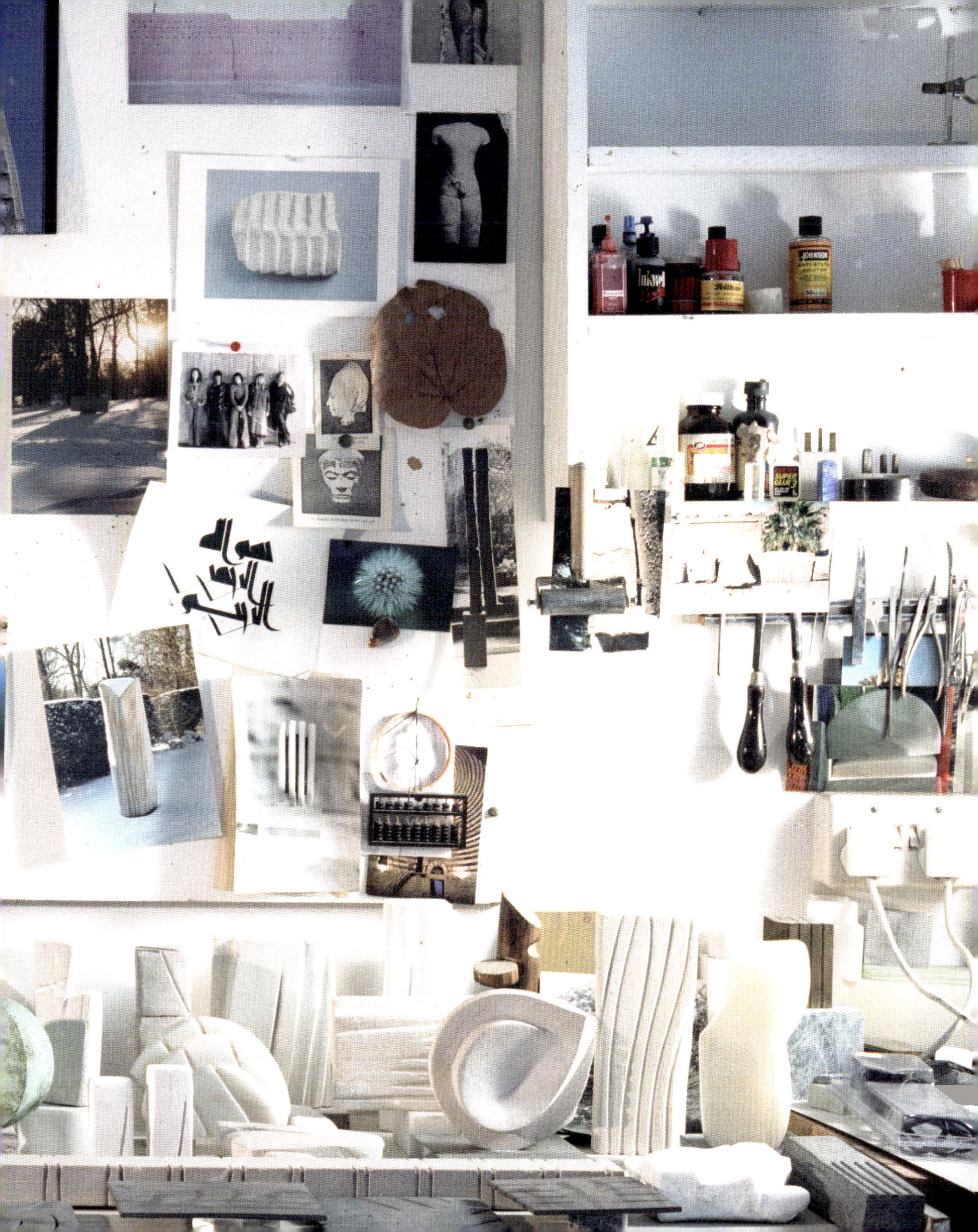
JOHNSON

50 **Gingko**, 1989 Aurora marble, 97·8 × 41·3 × 41·3 cm (39 × 16 × 16 in) The Estate of Kim Lim

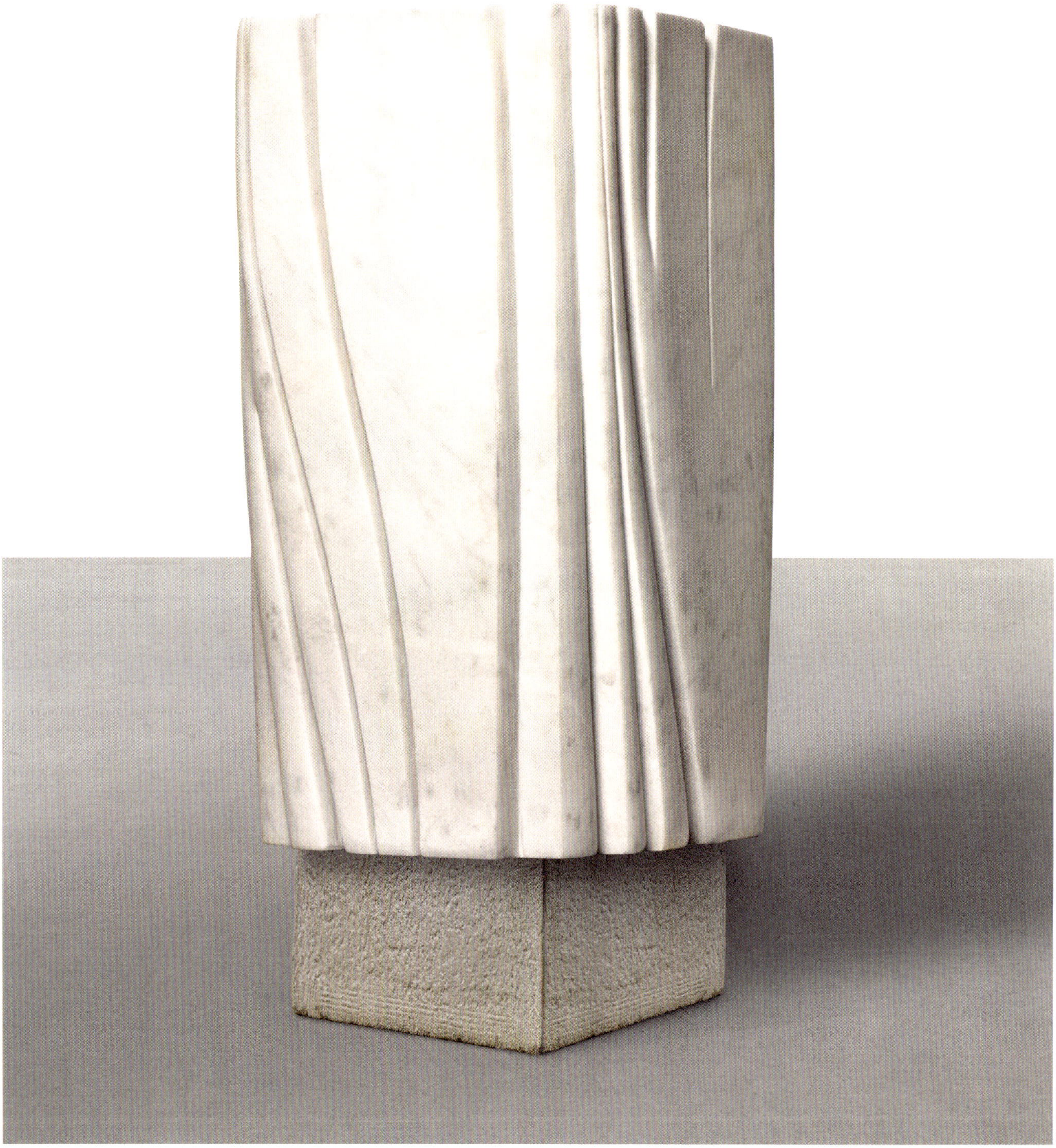

Hammad Nasar

An Invitation to Play: 'Quiet Mischief' and 'Slipperiness' in the Work of Kim Lim

A blown-up photograph of Kim Lim's studio wall (fig.49) anchored her presentation in the exhibition *A Century of the Artist's Studio: 1920–2020* at the Whitechapel Gallery (2022).[1] Lim's 'studio corner' in the exhibition was adjacent to similar displays of Barbara Hepworth's and Henry Moore's studios. In contrast to the photographs of these larger-than-life artists at work on one or two specific works, Lim's studio wall was a window into an expansive imagined world, within which her own presence could be easily missed. We glimpse this presence through a small, often-reproduced, photograph showing her among the five women selectors for the 1978 Hayward Annual (the others being Rita Donagh, Liliane Lijn, Tess Jaray and Gillian Wise Ciobotaru; fig.51).[2] Around this anchor in art history and friendship are a mixture of photographs of temple architecture, Lim's own sculptures, Arabic calligraphy and objects from museum displays taken during her travels across the Mediterranean to Japan, and then a number of objects closer to home (a yellowed leaf) as well as casual photographs capturing sunlight through trees and her youthful sons.

In the photograph, below the pinned images and objects on the studio wall, is a dense display of maquettes – mostly of carved stone. In the Whitechapel Gallery's exhibition, a selection of the same *real* maquettes ranging in size from 7 cm to 15 cm were positioned in front of the studio wall photograph on a low display case, and next to the carved marble sculpture *Gingko* (1989; fig.50). This arrangement reminds us of the human scale of Lim's work and, in dialogue with Lim's photographs, underlines its timeless power, which despite its often modest scale, demands 'monument-sized attention'.[3]

Running in parallel with the Whitechapel exhibition that showed Lim in dialogue with Hepworth and Moore around ideas of making was the Barbican Art Gallery's *Postwar Modern: New Art in Britain 1945–65* (2022) – an ambitious exhibitionary reframing of British art history.[4] Here Lim's four works in wood – *Muse* (1959; fig.10), *Chess Piece I* (1960; figs 2 and 9), *Chess Piece II* (1960) and *Ronin* (1963; fig.18) – were placed in the centre of a room of paintings by Lim's near-contemporaries Gillian Ayres, Frank Bowling, Patrick Heron and Anwar Jalal Shemza. This constellation underpinned the curators' argument

51 'A Biassed Show–Women Take Over The Hayward', *The Sunday Times Magazine*, 20 August 1978 The Estate of Kim Lim

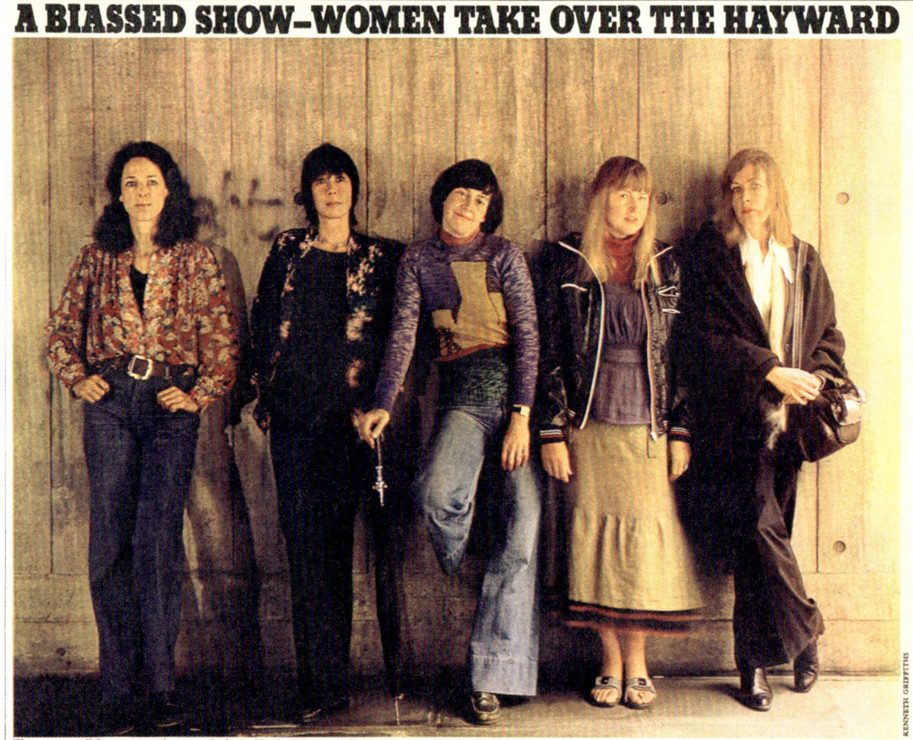

A BIASSED SHOW–WOMEN TAKE OVER THE HAYWARD

KENNETH GRIFFITHS

The group—all five women photographed outside the Hayward Gallery. From left to right: Tess Jaray, Kim Lim, Liliane Lijn, Gillian Wise Ciobotaru and Rita Donagh

that 'a feeling of form and space' was emerging from the mid-1950s in Britain – with war's dark shadow giving way to 'lightness and saturated colour'.[5]

The placement of Lim's work in dialogue with that of Hepworth and Moore at the Whitechapel can be seen as a curatorial tilt at the canon of 20th-century British sculpture. The centrality of her work to the 'Liberated Form and Colour' room at the Barbican was an even more direct attempt to make space for artists like Lim (but also Bowling and Shemza), whose work has often been contained within frames of 'biography, geography and difference',[6] and whose position in British art history remains 'at best slippery'.[7]

The cumulative effect of the Barbican and Whitechapel exhibitions (both 2022), closely following a display of Lim's prints and sculptures at Tate Britain (2020–21),[8] suggests an institutional urgency to make her position 'unslippery' – to locate the work of Kim Lim in the narratives of Britain's art history. That this latest flurry of activity is happening in Wakefield in 2023 for Lim's first UK museum survey in over twenty years, and in the run-up to the artist's forth-coming retrospective at the National Gallery Singapore (2024), suggests a tension, or at least a friendly competition, for art-historical sovereignty of artists with hyphenated identities.[9]

On this journey through exhibition histories, it is easy to forget the work itself. The aforementioned trio of London presentations of Lim's work, arriving so soon after each other like proverbial buses, brings our attention to her unique visual vocabulary, her exploration of rhythm, and her use of light and space as materials. I have written before about how these areas of investigation ran across her earlier work in prefabricated wood, steel and fibreglass, her later sculptures in carved stone and her work on paper.[10] Here, drawing from these earlier readings, I would like to suggest that this quality of 'slipperiness' is not confined to Lim's art-historical legacy, but is inherent to the invitation to 'play' that is integral to her work.

Lim spoke of space as a 'physical substance' that her sculptures 'punctuate'.[11] But her 'punctuation' of space, and direction of light and shadow, were playful – a movable feast rather than a predetermined set of rules. We can track this playfulness across her work over multiple decades. *Plus I*, *II* and *III* (all 1966; figs 52–4) reassemble similar constituent parts in aluminium into different shapes. The *Intervals*, *Link* and *Interstices* series (1973–7; (figs 56 and 57, fig 84) are serial arrangements of open-ended, modular structures of wood and acrylic that allow an infinite variety of presentation. With no obvious orientation (top and bottom, or front and back), many of them can be displayed on the floor or against the wall – and, for *Intervals*, at different angles between the spines and prongs of their components. The *Spiral* series (1983; fig.55) of sculptures in Portland stone form incomplete circles that allow contraction and expansion, and have been shown in gallery spaces, under trees and over water.

Lim's installations of her works, on their own or in dialogue with each other, such as in the 1977 Hayward Annual exhibition, demonstrate her interest in using the exhibition as an event to 'play' with light and space (fig.57). This exploration can be seen equally clearly across her works on paper, as in the screenprint *Intervals* (1972; fig.58) which uses multiple layers at different angles to create the optical effect of depth at the centre where the slat-like forms intersect.

While Lim's display at Tate Britain reflected the importance she placed on her printmaking practice ('the two activities – making sculpture and printmaking – are of equal importance to me'),[12] an evaluation of her oeuvre has suffered from a Eurocentric hierarchy of practice that places painting and sculpture above works on paper. For instance, neither the Whitechapel nor the Barbican featured her works on paper. The relationship of Lim's works on paper to her sculptures is full of possibility for further study. For example, her *Ladder* series of prints made in the early 1970s, such as *Ladder, Series 2* (1972; fig.44) and *Ladder Series 5* (1974; fig.59), suggest Lim was testing ideas on paper before working them out as sculptures such as the painted wood piece *Untitled* (1972; fig.60). These *Ladder* works are strikingly similar to the structural forms we see in *Intervals I* and *II* (1973; fig.57).

52 **Plus I**, 1966 aluminium, 26·5 × 25·5 × 7 cm (5 × 13 × 3 in) The Estate of Kim Lim

53 **Plus II**, 1966 aluminium, 11 × 34·5 × 7 cm (3 × 10 × 10 in) The Estate of Kim Lim

54 **Plus III**, 1966 aluminium, 13·5 × 34 × 7 cm (4 × 14 × 3 in) The Estate of Kim Lim

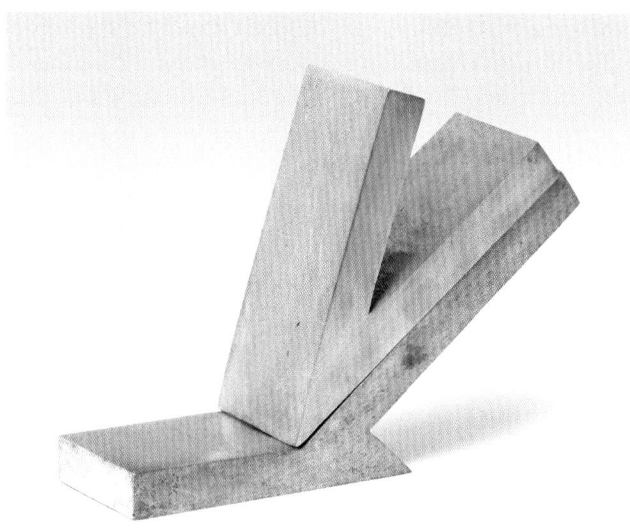

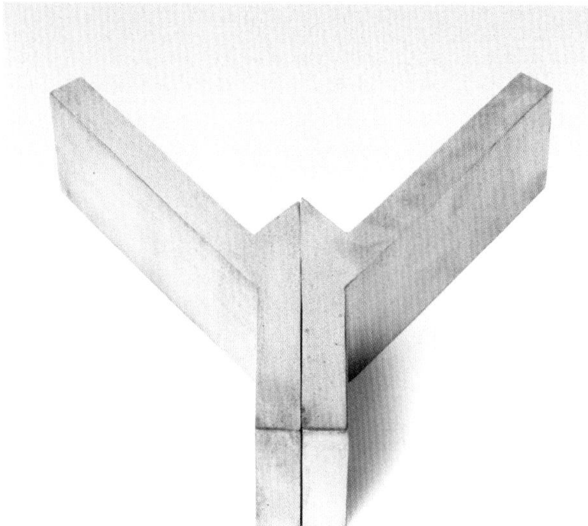

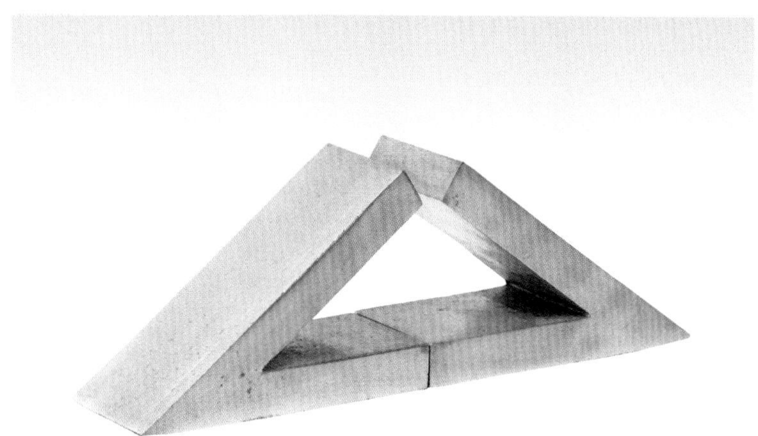

55 **Spiral II**, 1983 Portland stone, approx. 200 cm (79 in) radius
The Estate of Kim Lim

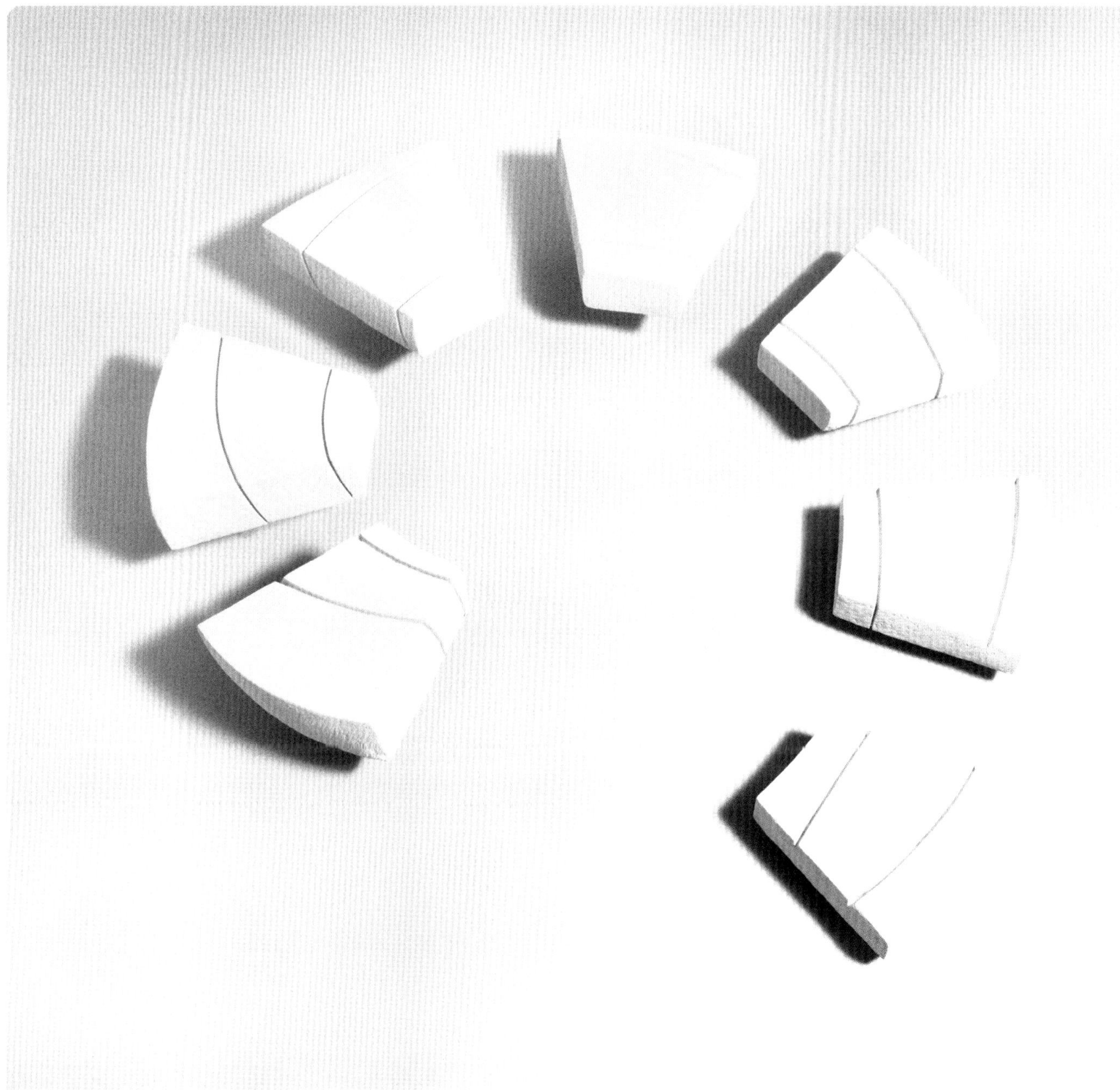

56 **Link II**, 1975 acrylic and wood, 383 × 12·8 × 2·2 cm (151 × 5 × 1 in) The Estate of Kim Lim

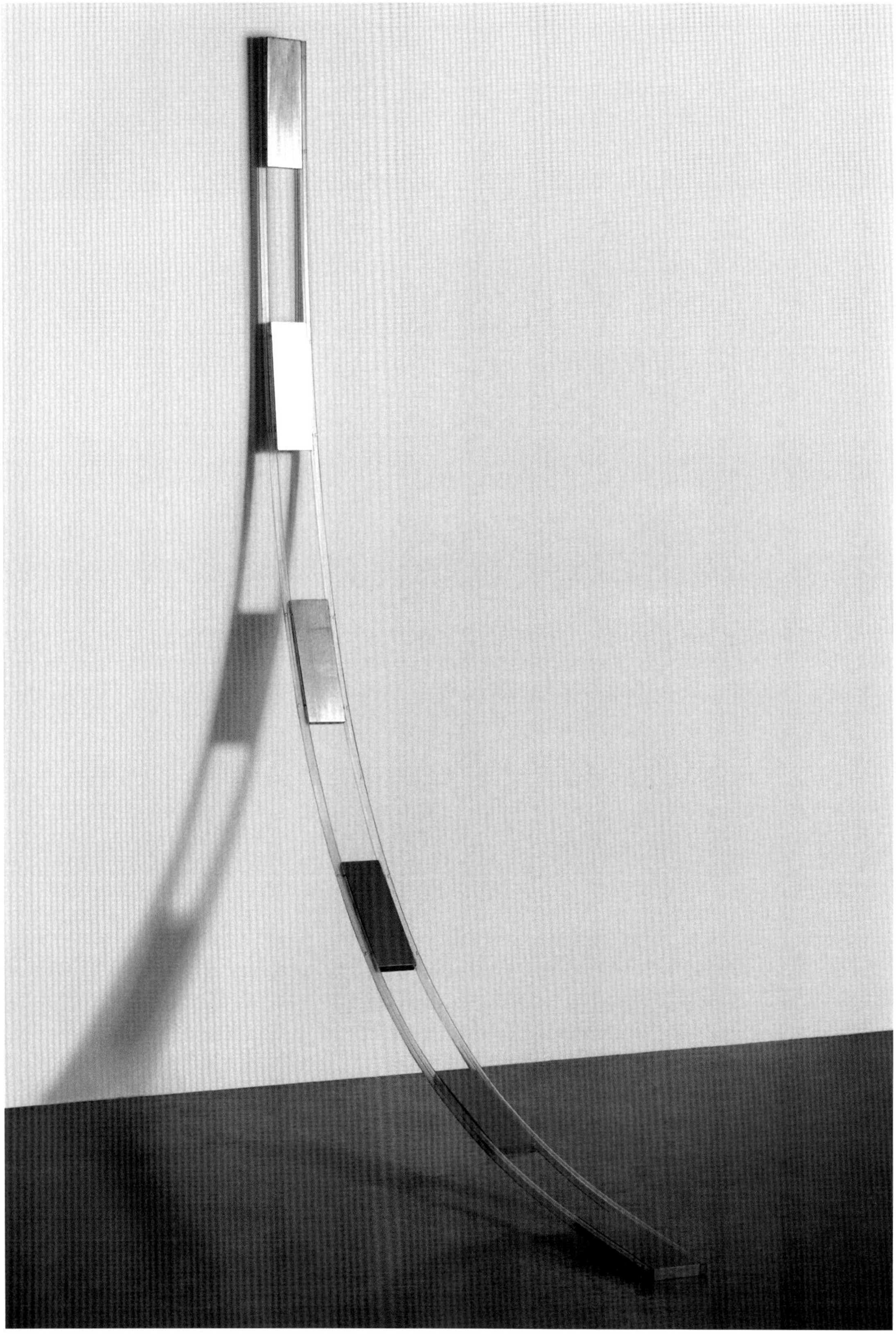

57 Artist's photograph of the Hayward Annual exhibition, Hayward Gallery, London, 1977, showing (from left to right): **Link II** (1975), **Intervals II** (1973), **Intervals I** (1973), **Intervals II** (1973), 1977 The Estate of Kim Lim

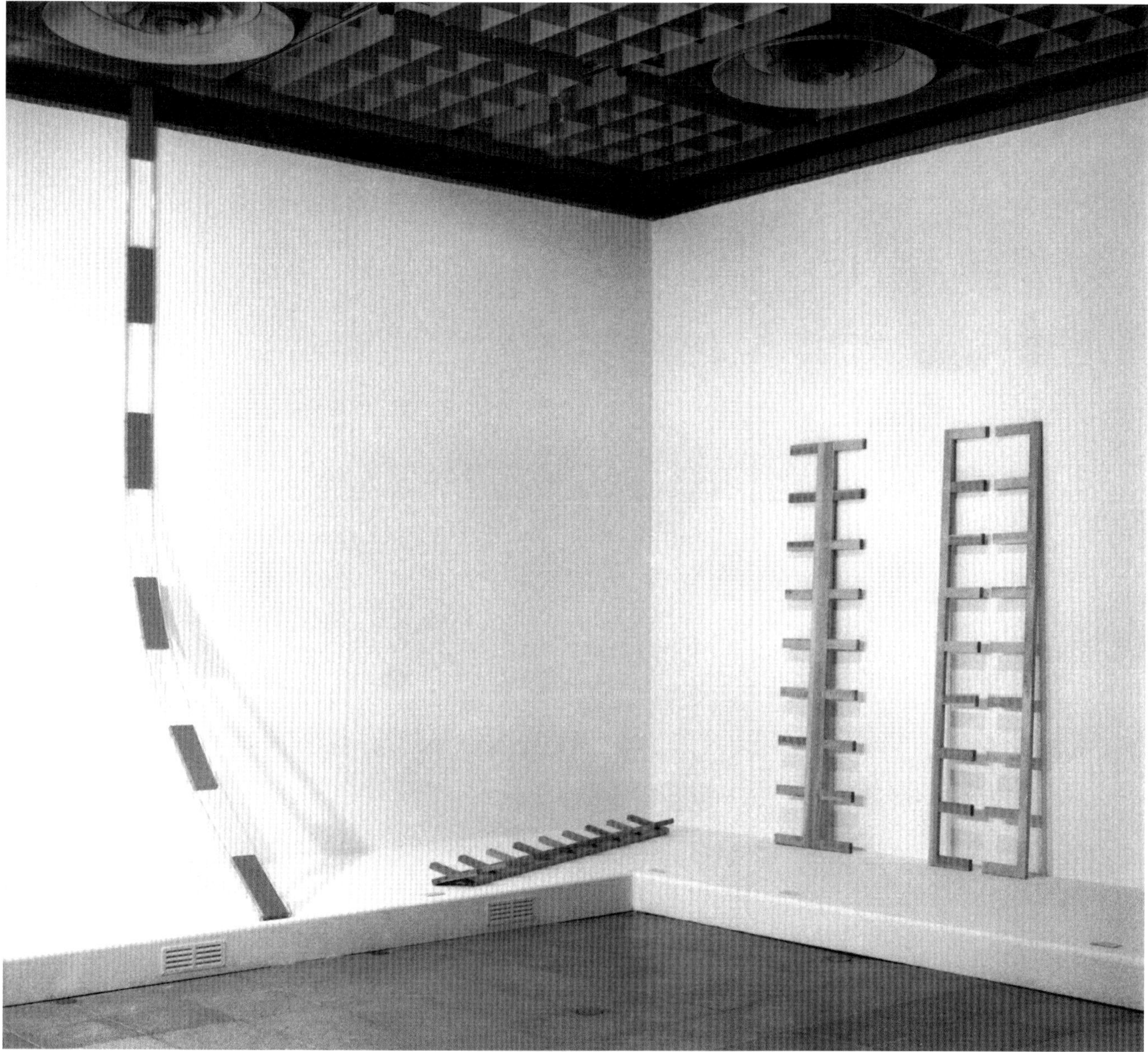

58 **Intervals Series**, 1972 screenprint on acrylic, 45 × 45 cm (18 × 18 in) The Estate of Kim Lim

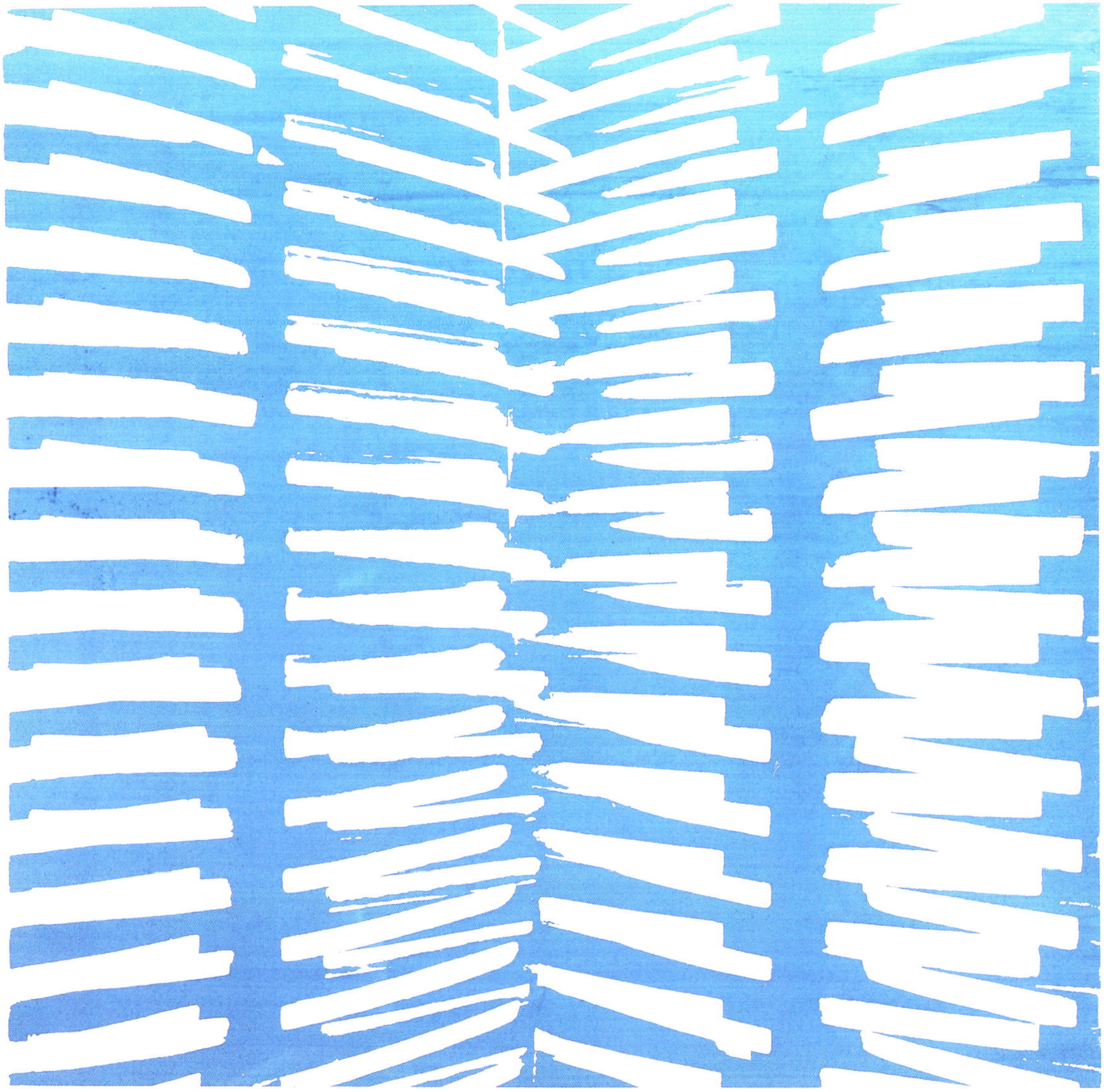

The multiple meanings of 'play' allow us to toggle between play as participation in a game and as performance on a musical instrument. Music was a touchstone for Lim's ideas of structure and rhythm. She once described in an interview the similarities between the composition of music and her sculptural forms, remarking 'how you have a kind of note ... the way it's repeated, and a reprise, and the intervals'.[13] This engagement can be glimpsed through some of her work titles, for instance *A Minor* (1979; fig.61), '*C Major*' (1979), *Timeshift* (1993) or *Syncopation 2* (1995; fig.62). As I have previously suggested, the prints too can be read 'as musical scores that Lim *performs* in her future sculptures; often producing, as seen above, multiple versions of the same work'.[14]

In this way, the exhibition of each sculptural work in new arrangements and contexts, like a musical performance, simultaneously allows for variation in play from the exhibition maker (artist or curator), and also invites perceptual engagement from the viewer to explore the work's possible variations (reconfiguration, reorientation, contraction or expansion). Lim's works want to be played with. That is their 'quiet mischief'.[15]

Notes

1 *A Century of the Artist's Studio: 1920–2020* was curated by Iwona Blazwick with Dawn Ades, Inês Costa, Richard Dyer, Hammad Nasar and Candy Stubbs at Whitechapel Gallery, London (24 February–5 June 2022).

2 More information about this exhibition can be found in Wenny Teo's chapter for this publication.

3 Hammad Nasar, 'Vectors of the New in Postwar Art in Britain,' in Jane Alison (ed.), *Postwar Modern: New Art in Britain 1945–65*, exhibition catalogue (London: Prestel Verlag & Barbican Art Gallery, 2022), p.23.

4 The exhibition was curated by Jane Alison with Charlotte Flint and Hilary Floe at the Barbican Art Gallery, London (March–June 2022). I was one of the exhibition's advisors, alongside Indie A. Choudhury, Ben Highmore, Lynda Nead, Gregory Salter and Sarah Victoria Turner.

5 Charlotte Flint, 'Liberated Form and Space', in *Postwar Modern: New Art in Britain 1945–65*, p.257.

6 *Speech Acts: Reflection – Imagination – Repetition* at Manchester Art Gallery (2018–19), curated by Hammad Nasar with Kate Jesson, was part of, and in conversation with, the 'Black Artists and Modernism' (BAM) project, led by artist Sonia Boyce. A PDF of the gallery guide for *Speech Acts* is available at https://manchesterartgallery.org/wp-content/uploads/2021/11/BAM-Speech-Acts-Guide14.pdf.

7 Nasar, 'Vectors of the New in Postwar Art in Britain', p.23.

8 *Kim Lim: Carving and Printing* was curated by Elena Crippa at Tate Britain, London (2020–21). It is also worth noting the catalysing effect of the exhibition *Kim Lim*, curated by Darren Leak and Bianca Chu, at SI2, London (September–November 2018).

9 For a consideration of this phenomenon and its impact on the possibilities for British art history in relation to Rasheed Araeen and Li Yuan-chia, see Hammad Nasar, 'Notes from the Field: Navigating the Afterlife of the *Other Story*', *Asia Art Archive* (1 April 2015), https://aaa.org.hk/en/ideas/ideas/notes-from-the-field-navigating-the-afterlife-of-the-other-story.

10 This text draws on my earlier essays, including: 'Resisting Resolution: Kim Lim's Playful Stillness', in Bianca Chu and Darren Leak (eds), *Kim Lim* (London: Sotheby's, 2018), pp 94–101, and 'Vectors of the New in Postwar Art in Britain', in *Postwar Modern: New Art in Britain 1945–65*, pp 21–7.

11 Typewritten notes from the Kim Lim archive, reproduced in Chu and Leak, *Kim Lim*, p.58.

12 Kim Lim, quoted in Tate's catalogue entry on the work, accessible on Tate website, https://www.tate.org.uk/art/artworks/lim-intervals-ii-t02002.

13 Kim Lim, Interview with Cathy Courtney, London, 20 October 1995, *National Life Stories: Artists' Lives* (London: British Library, 1995), C466/51, transcript, p.76.

14 Nasar, 'Resisting Resolution', p.101. This reading has been informed by the experience of curating presentations of Kim Lim's prints in conjunction with her sculptures in *Speech Acts: Reflection – Imagination – Repetition* at Manchester Art Gallery (2018–19), and *Structures of Meaning | Architectures of Perception*, curated with Sophie Persson, Abu Dhabi Art at Manarat Al Saadiyat (November 2018 – January 2019).

15 Nasar, 'Resisting Resolution', p.95.

59 **Ladder Series 5**, 1974 etching on paper, 77·5 × 51·5 cm (30 × 20 in) The Estate of Kim Lim

60 **Untitled**, 1972 painted wood, 176 × 63 × 2 cm (69 × 25 × 1 in) The Estate of Kim Lim

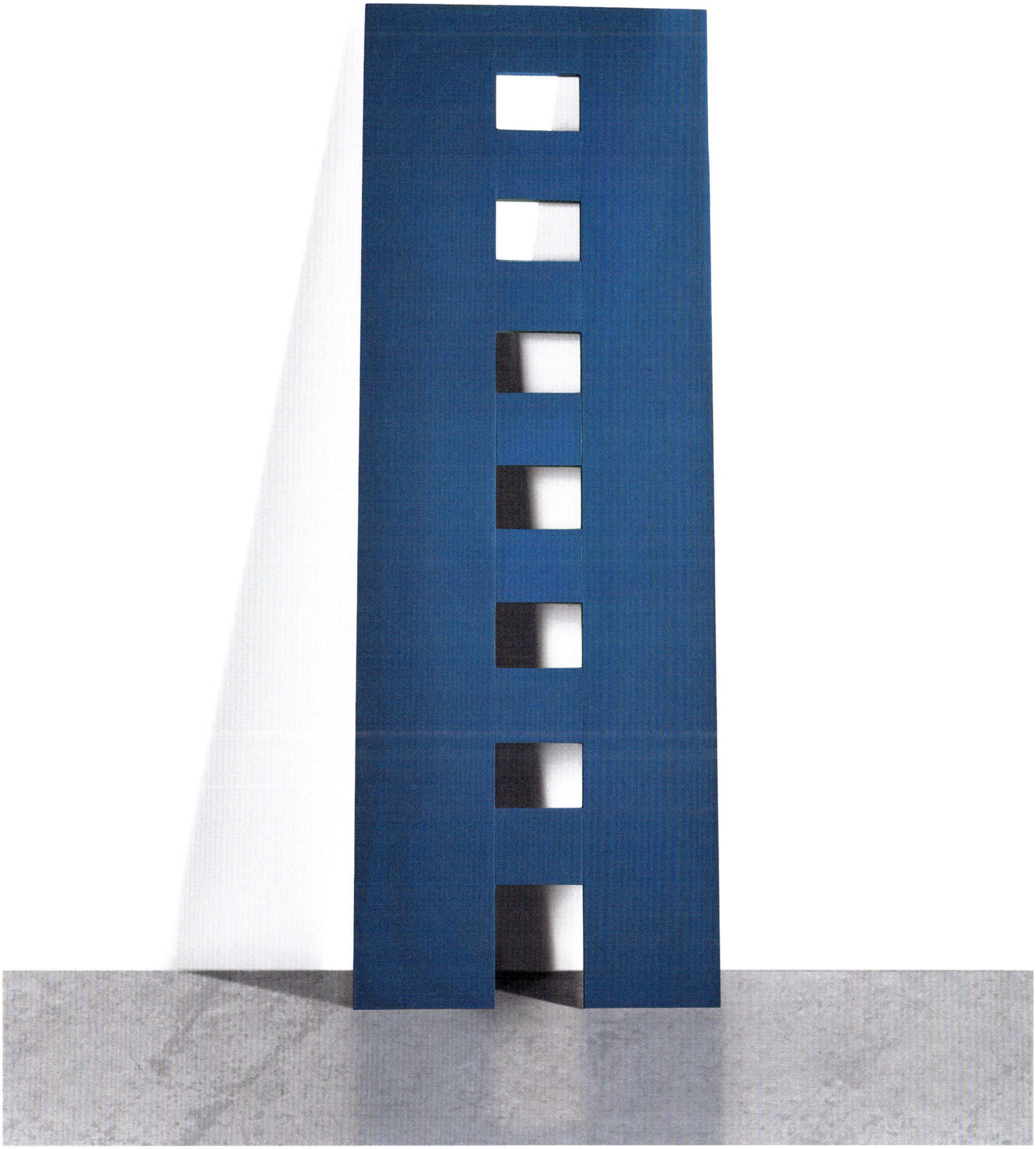

61 **A Minor**, 1979 woodcut on paper, 48 × 48 cm (19 × 19 in) The Estate of Kim Lim

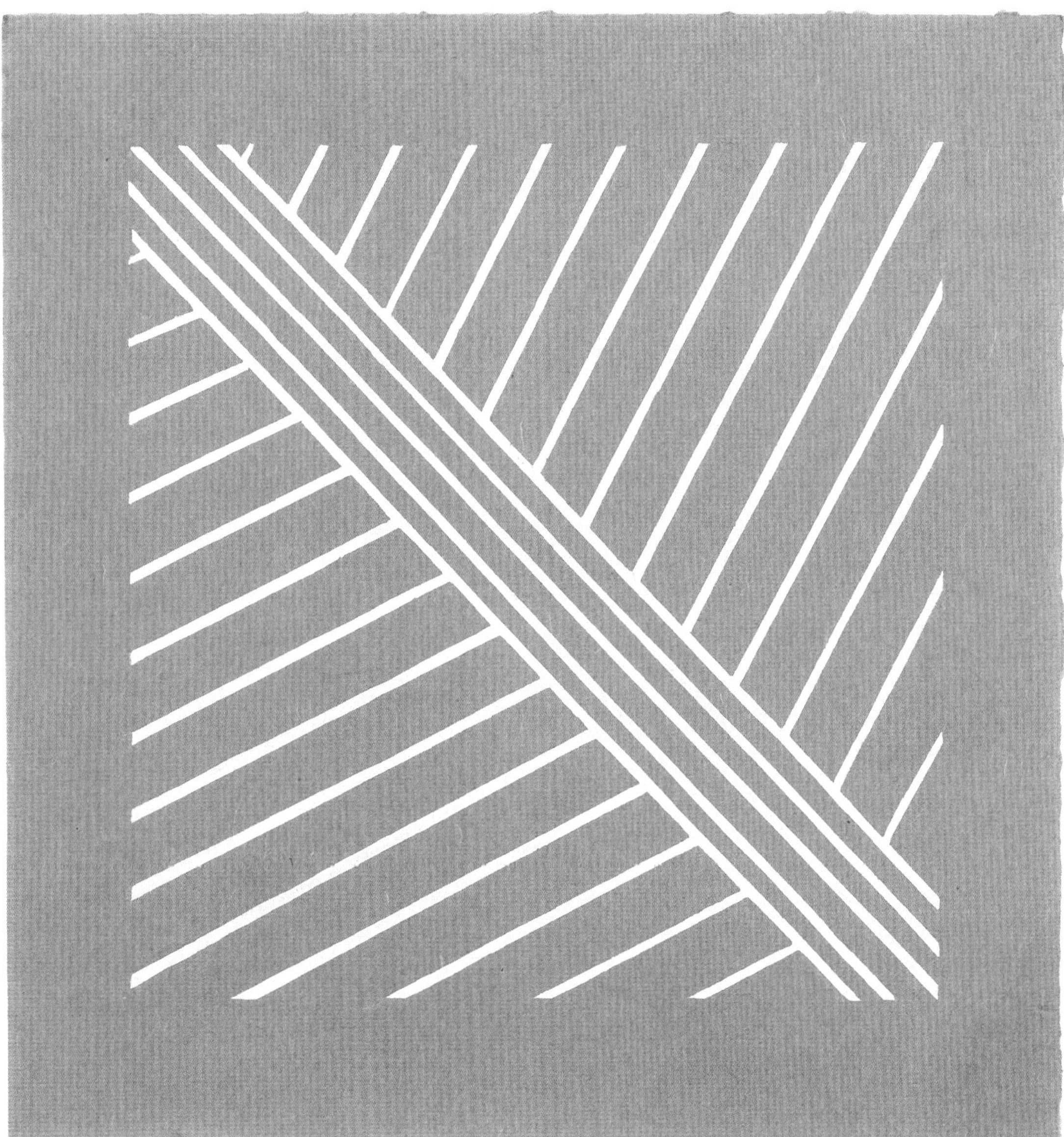

62 **Syncopation 2**, 1995 slate, 40·5 × 44·5 × 1·5 cm (16 × 17 × 1 in)
The Estate of Kim Lim

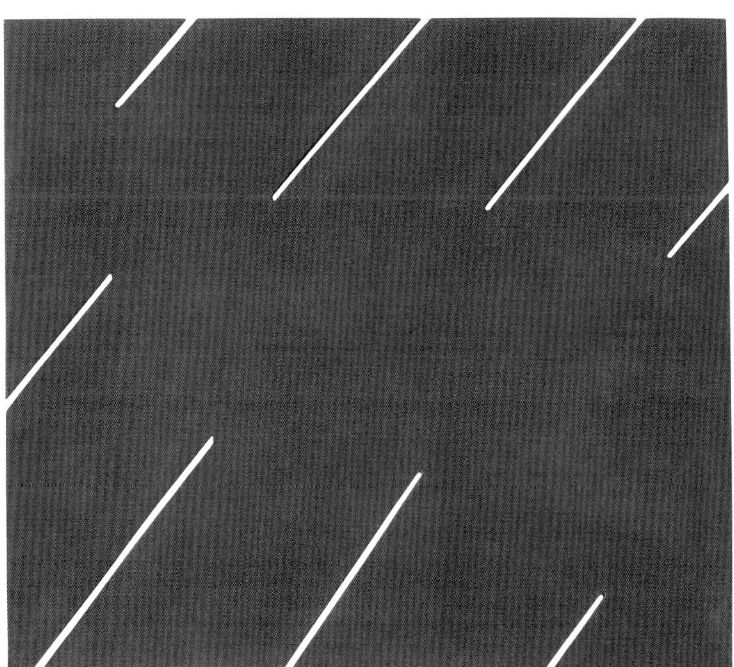

63 **Slate Relief**, 1995 slate, 46 × 46 × 5 cm (18 × 18 × 2 in)
The Estate of Kim Lim

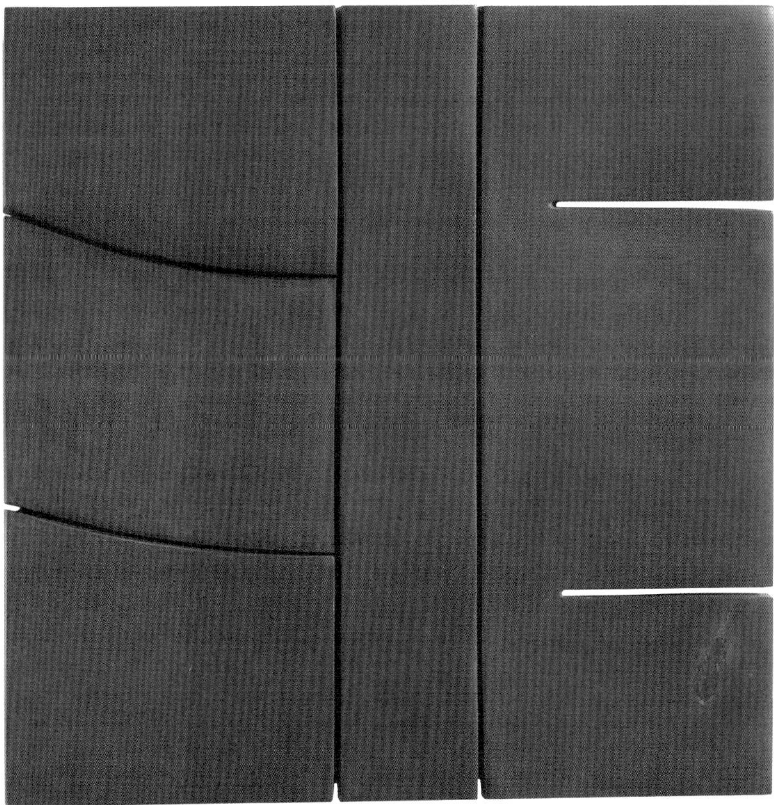

64 **Twice**, 1966 brass, 127 × 129·5 × 20·3 cm (50 × 51 × 8 in) The Estate of Kim Lim

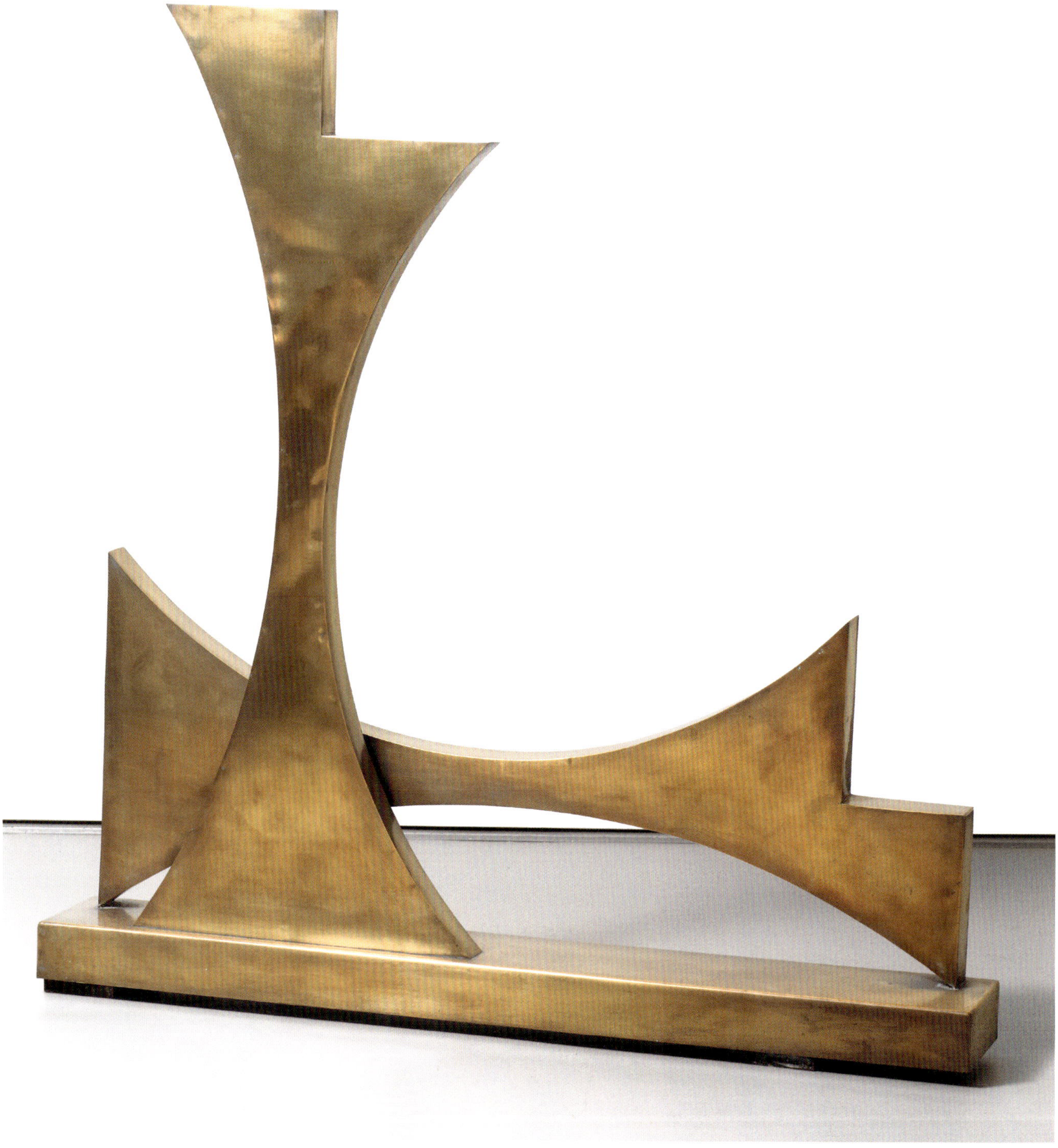

Joleen Loh and Adele Tan

'Call and Response': Asia and Kim Lim

The following is a dialogue between the two curators of Lim's upcoming retrospective at National Gallery Singapore, discussing the artist, her works in the collection and the presence of Asia in her art.

Adele Tan (AT): Although Kim Lim is now largely received as a British artist, audiences have been very receptive and curious towards her bi-cultural background – having been born in Singapore and growing up in wartime Malaya – because of the embedded presence of Asia in her works. There appears to be a form of 'call and response' between the East and West that has shaped her artistic thinking and practice. I use the musical term 'call and response', inspired by Lim's sustained referencing of musical motifs in her titles, such as her 1979 woodcuts *C Major* and *A Minor* (fig.61), and the prominence of time and intervals in her works. In music, call-and-response is a compositional technique similar to a conversation. A 'phrase' of music serves as the 'call', and is 'answered' by a different phrase of music that can be vocal or instrumental. This back-and-forth movement is how I see Asia recurring time and again in Lim's artistic development, and yet also contrapuntally, where more than one musical line plays concurrently – independent but harmonically related.

Joleen Loh (JL): Kim Lim used repetition, like in music, to build effects and sensations with analogous variations, accentuating not only surface patterns but basic shapes in multi-partite works. In her first solo exhibition at the Axiom Gallery in London in 1966, Lim debuted a group of wood and metal sculptures, that signalled her interest in conveying the richness of imagery through flat surfaces characterised by identical features on both sides of the plane. They are each distinct but nonetheless in conversation. Concave and convex shapes turn up as variants or memories of each other. For instance, the hemispherical forms in *Pegasus* (1962; fig.22) are echoed in *Borneo I* (1964), reiterated in works like *Candy* (1965; fig.65) and appear in the negative spaces of *Blue Note* (1966; fig.66) and *Twice* (1966; fig.64). It is tempting to exert a biographical

65 **Candy**, 1965 painted wood, 59 × 183 × 17 cm (23 × 72 × 7 in) Arts Council Collection, Southbank Centre, London

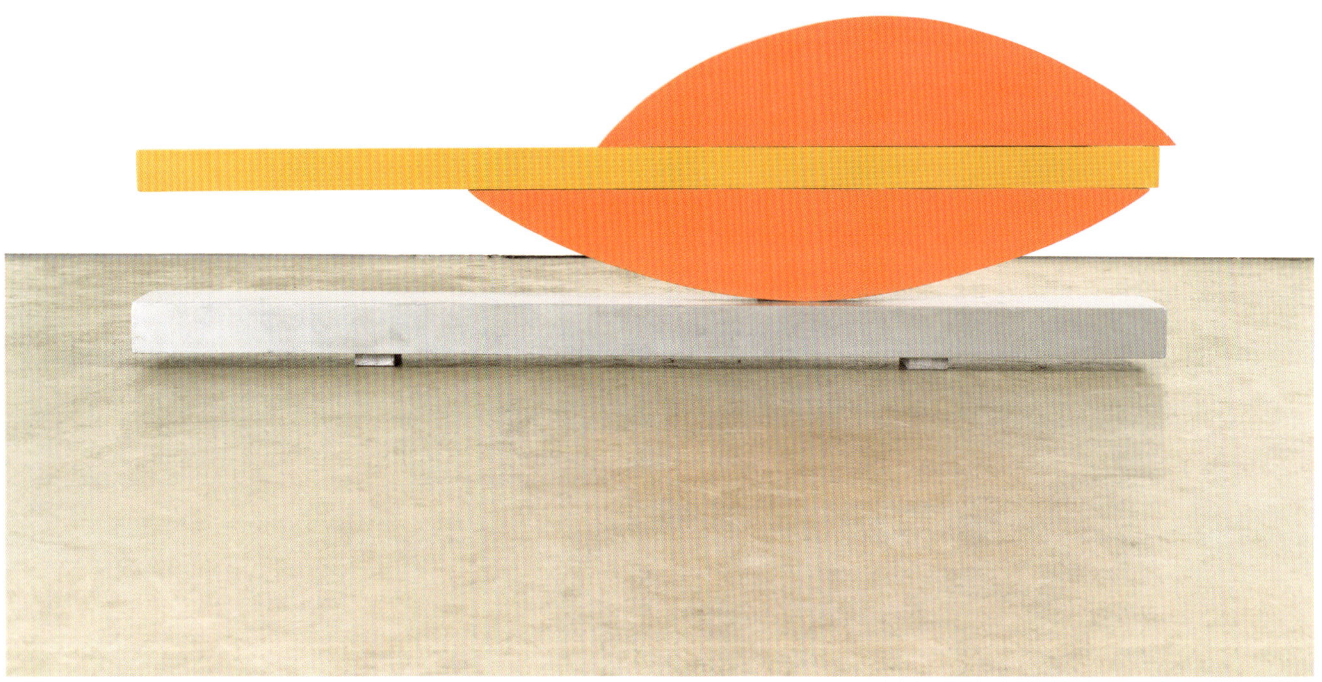

66 **Blue Note**, 1966 stainless steel, 124·5 × 45·7 cm (49 × 18 in) The Estate of Kim Lim

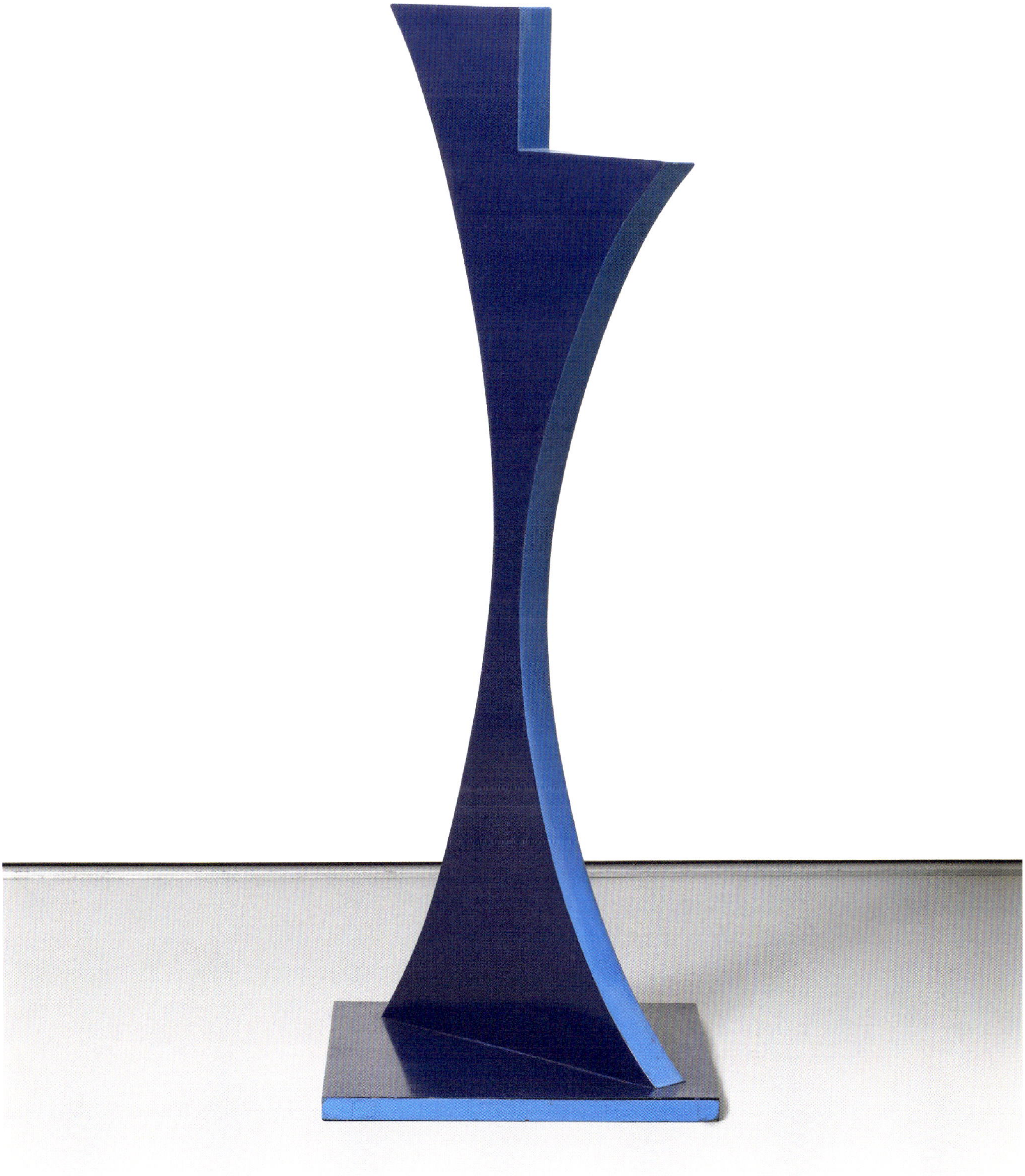

67 **Samurai I**, 1960 wood and stone, dimensions unknown

reading onto *Borneo I*, a life-sized painted steel sculpture with winged features that suggest a bird in flight. Lim's father had roots in Sarawak, Borneo. Yet Lim resisted biographical interpretations of her work, echoing the widespread anxiety felt by many diasporic artists in Britain that they would be pigeonholed by their nationality. To Lim, the effectiveness of this body of work lay in the succinctness of form and its multiple imaginative connotations. Ancient mythologies and cultural referents also enter her works. In earlier titles, there are nods to figures from Japanese history in *Shogun* (1960), *Samurai I* (1960; fig.67) and *Ronin* (1963; fig.18). Without any affixed meaning, these sculptures invite aesthetic contemplation and an engagement with them that is detached from human history.

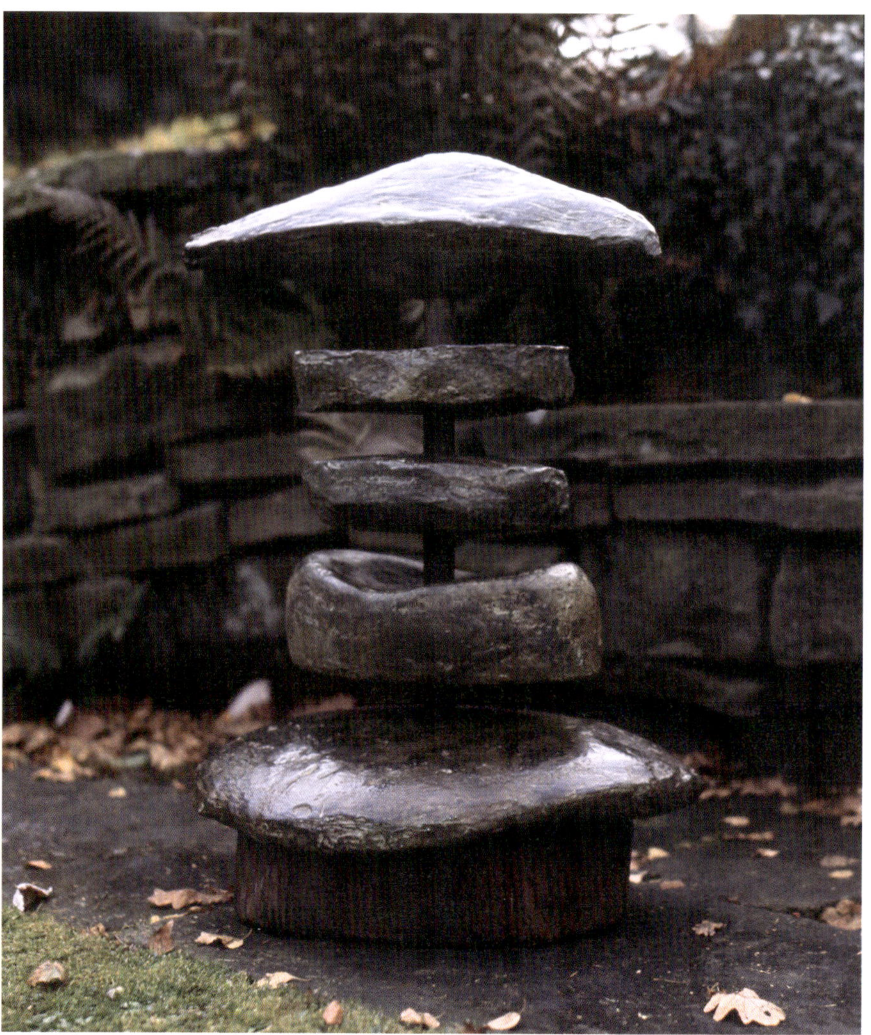

68 **Abacus**, 1959 plaster, wood and metal, 44·5 × 55·9 × 5.1 cm (18 × 22 × 2 in) National Gallery Singapore

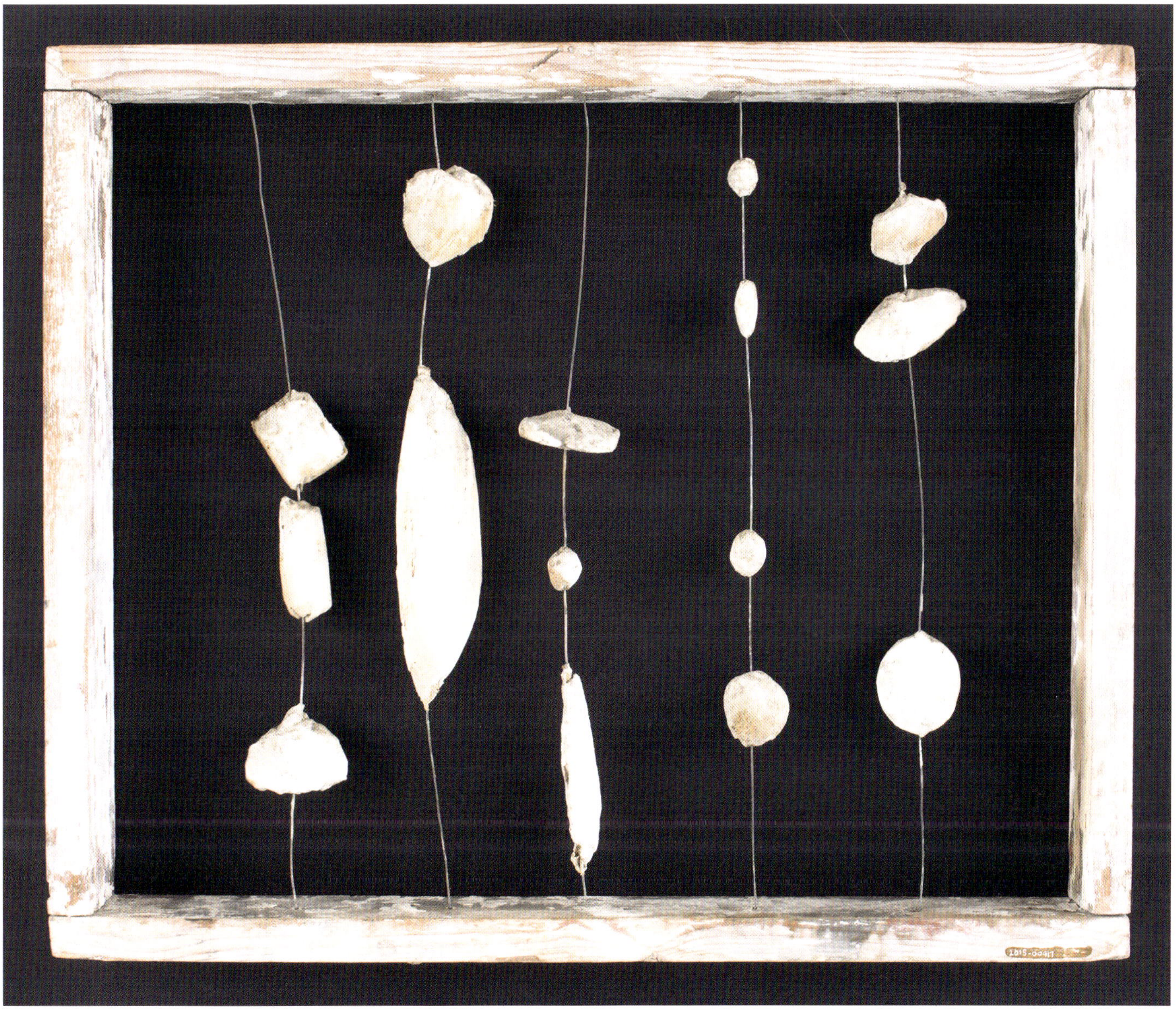

AT: Kim Lim's *Abacus* (fig.68) from 1959 is striking and instructive in this regard. There are two versions in different sizes and a charcoal drawing, acknowledging how a mundane instrument of business could also be a sculptural work of art. The abacus is a well-recognised counting frame to the Chinese, consisting of columns of movable strung beads and used to denote numbers for basic calculations, symbolic too of the merchant-class background of the artist's extended family in Singapore. Yet there is a different calculus at play. The artwork's title gives the artefact its cultural context but, without this referent, one could also easily register it as a child's counting toy or a celestial mobile. This shuttling between points recalls Kim Lim's flights between London and Singapore as a college student, whereof she said that 'you could stop off as many times as you like, as long as you were travelling vaguely in the direction of your destination'.[1] Europe and Asia were productive stops where art was always the eventual end point. Comparing her experiences in the two locations, she said that in London she found herself as an artist, losing herself in its millions of people, most of whom are far too busy to care what another does, compared with Singapore, where people 'can't help but know what you are doing', and are 'far too ready to leap to conclusions'.[2]

JL: In a way, Asia became more productive for Kim Lim once she had left it. She felt that Singapore was 'a very difficult place to be creative in', its smallness rendering it 'so hermetically sanitised it makes endeavours hard to develop'.[3] In 1954 Lim's move to London to study broadened her experiences of art beyond classical Chinese scroll paintings, ceramics and collections of ethnographic artefacts from Southeast Asia.[4] But at the Slade in the late 1950s, Lim did not wholly accept the canon of Western art either and questioned the linearity and Eurocentrism of accounts of art history that she was taught in school. Travel allowed her to make her own corrections, exploring museums, monuments and historic architectural sites across multiple cities in Europe and Asia while en route to visit family in Singapore – 'that was my art education, not art schools'.[5] These journeys, which also took her home to Singapore, layered with her own exposure to the British art world, expanded her frames of reference (fig.69). Her cosmopolitan visual language was informed by multiple aesthetic systems and vocabularies that drew on, for example, transnational geographical and mythological references.

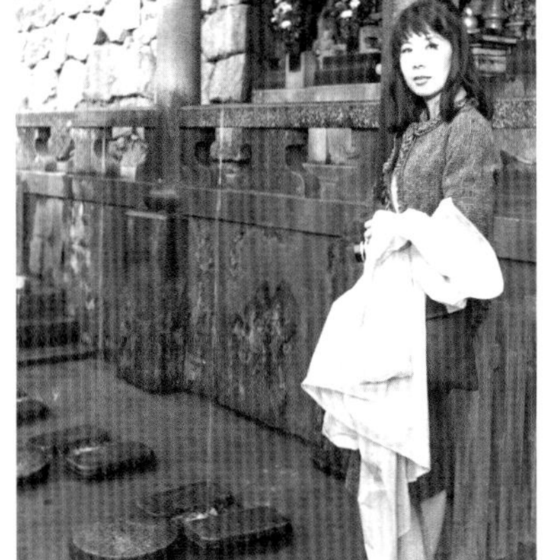

69 Kim Lim, *c.*1950s The Estate of Kim Lim

AT: There is a persistence of geographical nodes in her oeuvre. The regular, repetitive and rule-based timeless geometry of her wood-based sculptures of the 1970s, such as *Intervals I* and *II* (1973; fig.57), *Plus II* (1973; fig.53), *Bridge I* (1976) and *Stack* (1976), surprisingly meets the eruption of a sculpture like *Irrawaddy* (1979; fig.70), whose pinewood blocks appear knocked over like in a game of

70 **Irrawaddy**, 1979 pinewood, in 18 parts, each 81·3 × 10·2 × 5·1 cm (32 × 4 × 2 in) National Gallery Singapore

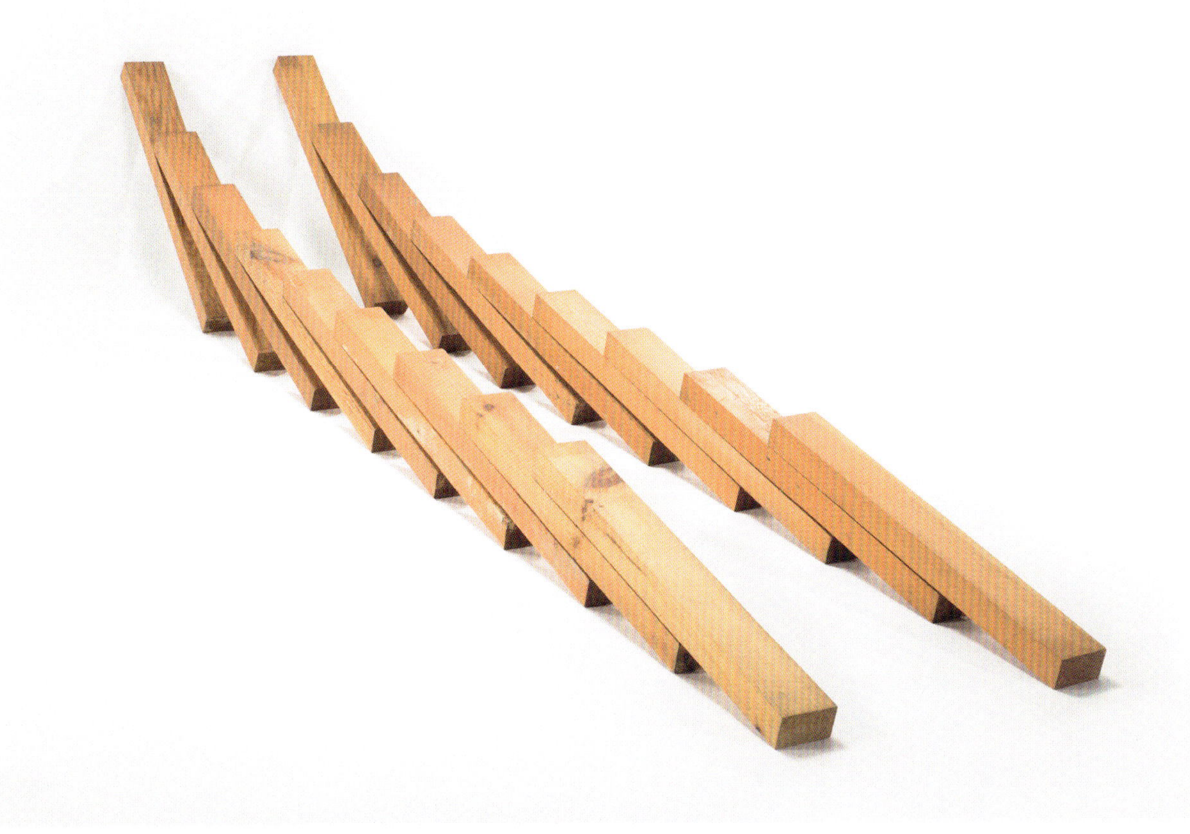

dominoes but which ever more effectively conjure up the power and magnificence of the waters of the Irrawaddy River that runs through what was then Burma and is now Myanmar.

JL: Travel and documentation were central features to Lim's way of life and to her artistic practice. Over decades, she amassed albums of photographs she took on these self-initiated travels across cities in countries including Cambodia, China, Indonesia, India, Italy, Japan, Malaysia and Turkey. She photographed architecture, monuments, sculptures and nature, often from multiple perspectives. Ancient sites and art of Asian civilisations, such as Angkor Wat in Cambodia, impressed her just as much as gardens and modern art in museums (fig.71). These transcultural reference points articulate her interests in the emotional registers of space, light, rhythm and shadow. The act of pinning the photographs onto the walls of her studio next to maquettes and documentation of her sculptures suggests the strong affinities between them, offering alternate genealogies for a sculptural language informed by a plurality of artistic traditions and ancient cultures.[6]

AT: Time and again Kim Lim thwarts our expectations. She introduces a similarly styled stone-based work to the minimal-looking *Spiral* series (1983, fig.55) but displaces its encircling lines into a sinuous sequence and calls it *Naga* (1984; fig.73). It is a title freighted with symbolic and narrative weight from Hindu-Buddhist traditions, a serpentine creature that bears both incredible danger and divinity and a popular sculptural element in temples across Cambodia, Laos, Thailand, Sri Lanka and India. But if one were to recall her early sculptures of the late 1950s and early 1960s, *Naga* follows in the footsteps of *Sphinx* (1959) and *Pegasus* (1962; fig.22). Perhaps *Naga* can be considered an offspring of the enigmatic *Sphinx* which, unlike conventional sculptures that hold a constant static form, is capable of growing and changing – a feature that would continue in Lim's series of works in the 1970s, such as *Interstices*, which could be arranged in various ways (figs 84 and 85).

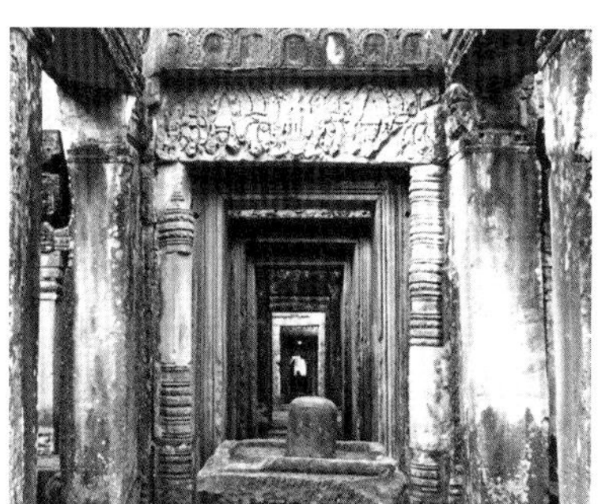

71 Kim Lim, Angkor Wat, Cambodia, 1962
The Estate of Kim Lim

JL: From 1979 on, as Lim moved to carving in stone, she wanted to introduce 'more freedom into the work' through 'dynamic rhythms of organic, structured forms'.[7] In *Langkawi* (1988; fig.72) serpentine striations course along the vertical marble column, its edges and profile softened with graining and gentle concavities that sink into its surfaces, implying the natural erosion or undulations of water. In works such as *Untitled* (1978; fig.74) and *Water Piece* (1979; fig.75) Lim sought to capture the organic flows and rhythms of water, taking points of reference from her memories of the extended periods of time spent by the sea in Penang, and of the torrential rains there and in Singapore.[8] Walking around *Langkawi*, we become aware of its different tactile sensibilities, as our eyes are drawn across its surfaces through incisions, fissures and tender gradations of light across its four sides. These subtle but complex surfaces in *Langkawi* are characteristic of Lim's later works in stone, where movement and rhythm deploy a kind of repetition similar to the structure of music, where notes may be repeated, reprised, punctuated by intervals. Many of her works revisited past ideas to discover new permutations, so perhaps we might also read them as metaphors for her own lived experiences and memories. She observed that she worked 'in a much more cyclic way' that was not a 'question of progressing or getting better' but of 'discovery and rediscovery', much like travelling, when one is able to visit a place twice and 'see totally different things because you are different and you're looking for something different'.[9]

AT: The Portland stone that was more visible in Kim Lim's sculptures of the earlier years of the 1980s (fig.77) gave way to an expanded repertoire of stones such as granite (fig.76), marble (fig.78) and then slate (figs 62 and 63). *Langkawi* belongs to the last decade of the artist's practice before her death from breast

72 **Langkawi**, 1988 white Sicilian marble, 120 × 27·9 × 17·8 cm (47 × 11 × 7 in)
Gift of Dr Arthur Lim Siew Ming. National Gallery Singapore

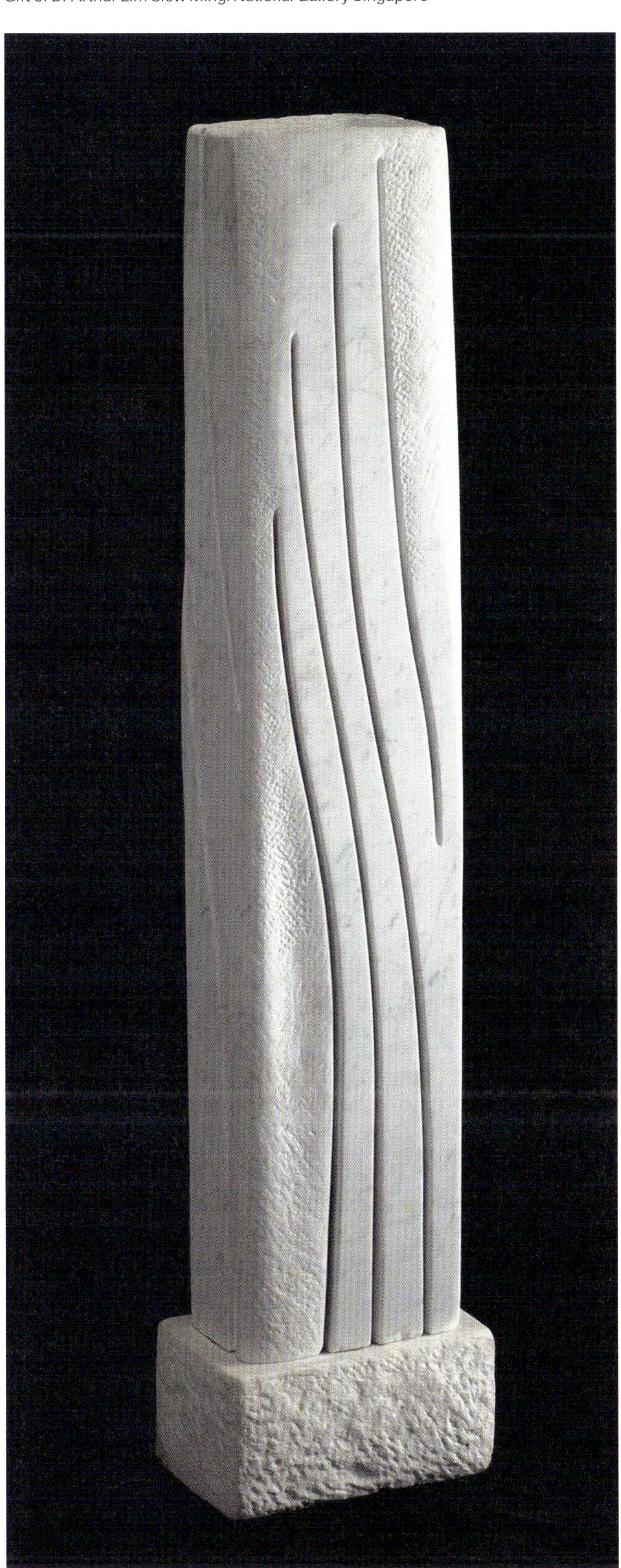

73 **Naga**, 1984 Portland stone, in seven parts, dimensions variable
National Gallery Singapore

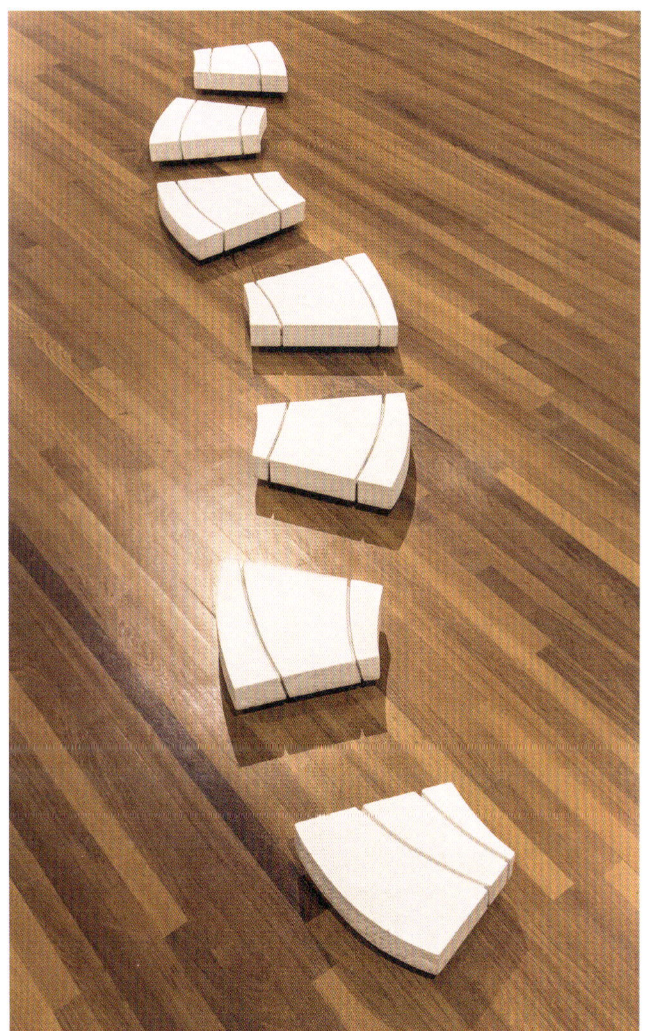

74 **Untitled**, 1978 paper, 45 × 45 cm (18 × 18 in) The Estate of Kim Lim

75 **Water Piece**, 1979 bronze, 51 × 48 × 10 cm (20 × 19 × 4 in) The Estate of Kim Lim

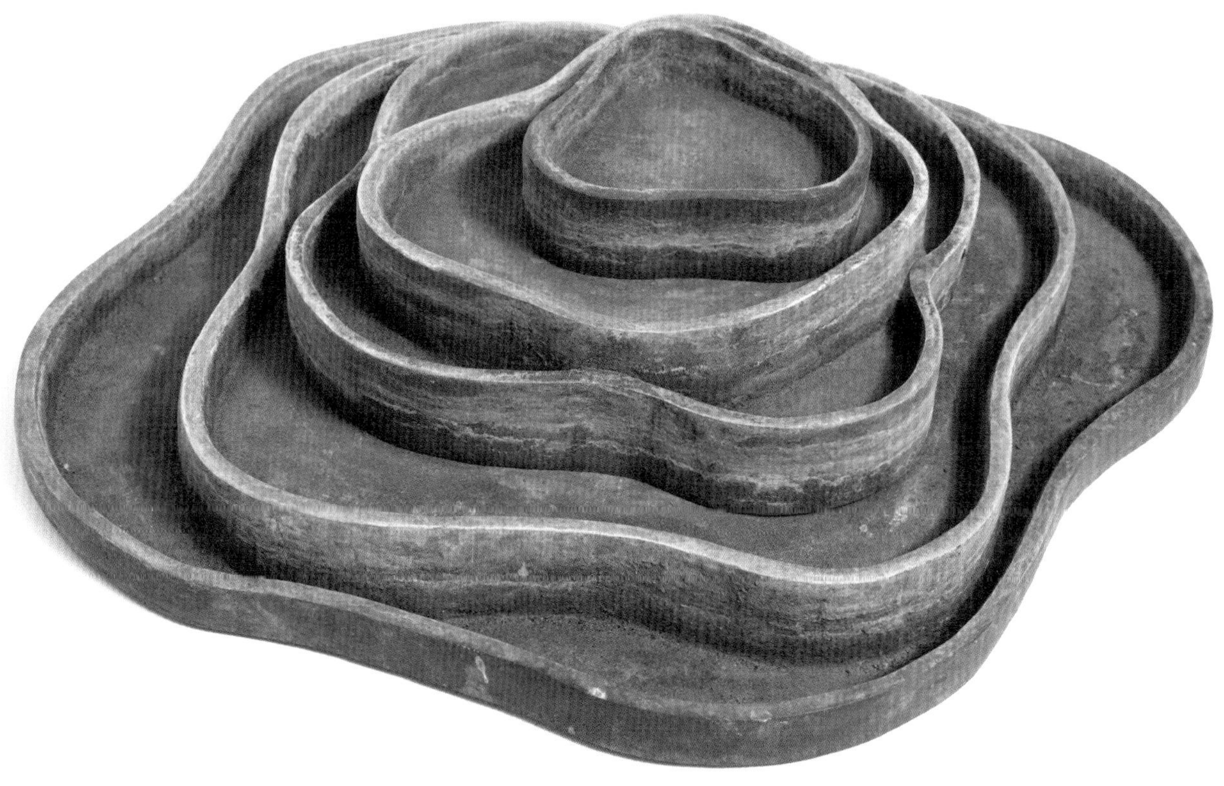

76 **Untitled II**, 1993–7 granite, 205·2 × 88·9 × 72.9 cm (81 × 35 × 29 in) The Estate of Kim Lim

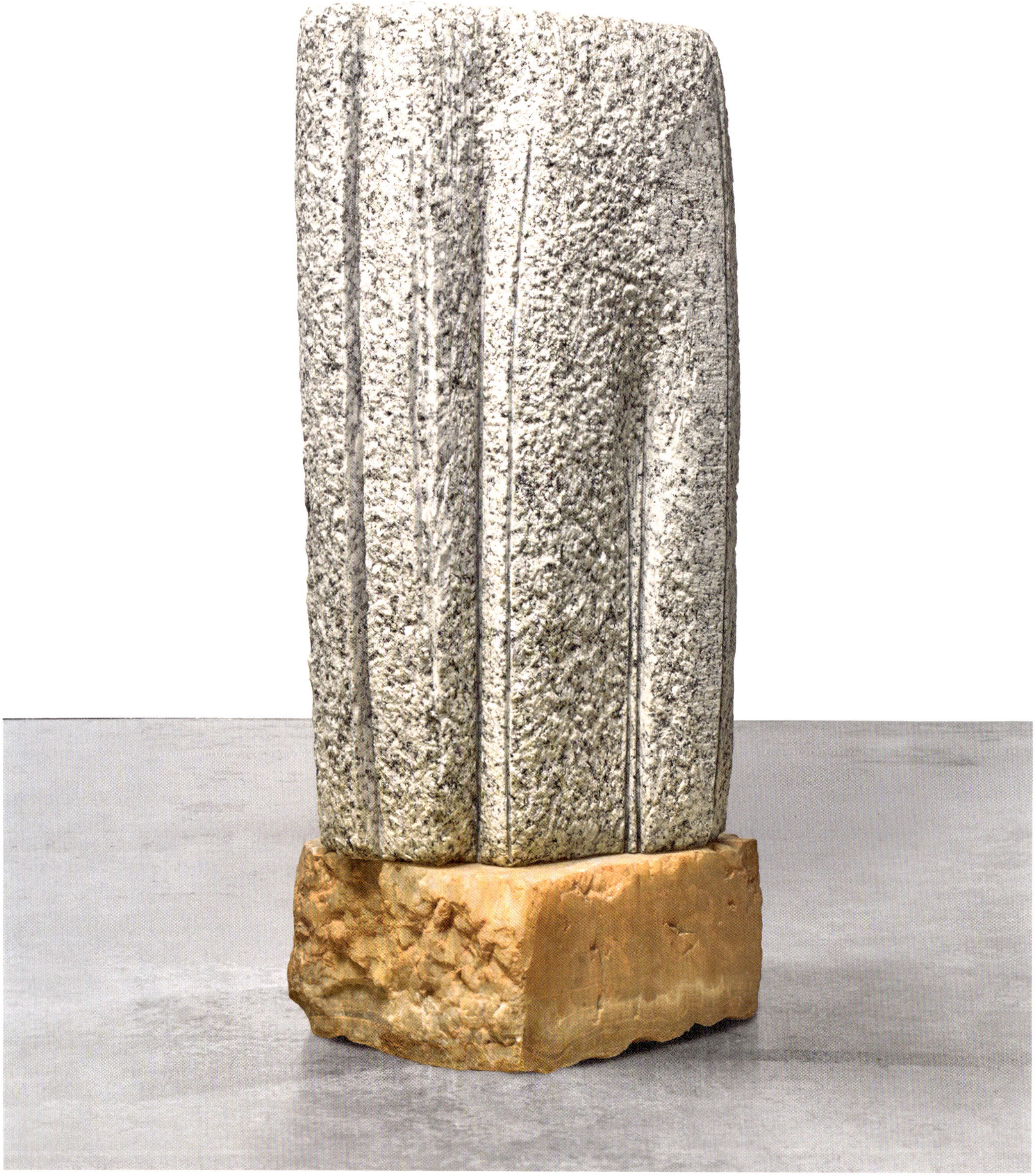

77 **Padma I**, 1983 Portland stone, 34 × 23 × 23 cm (13 × 9 × 9 in) The Estate of Kim Lim

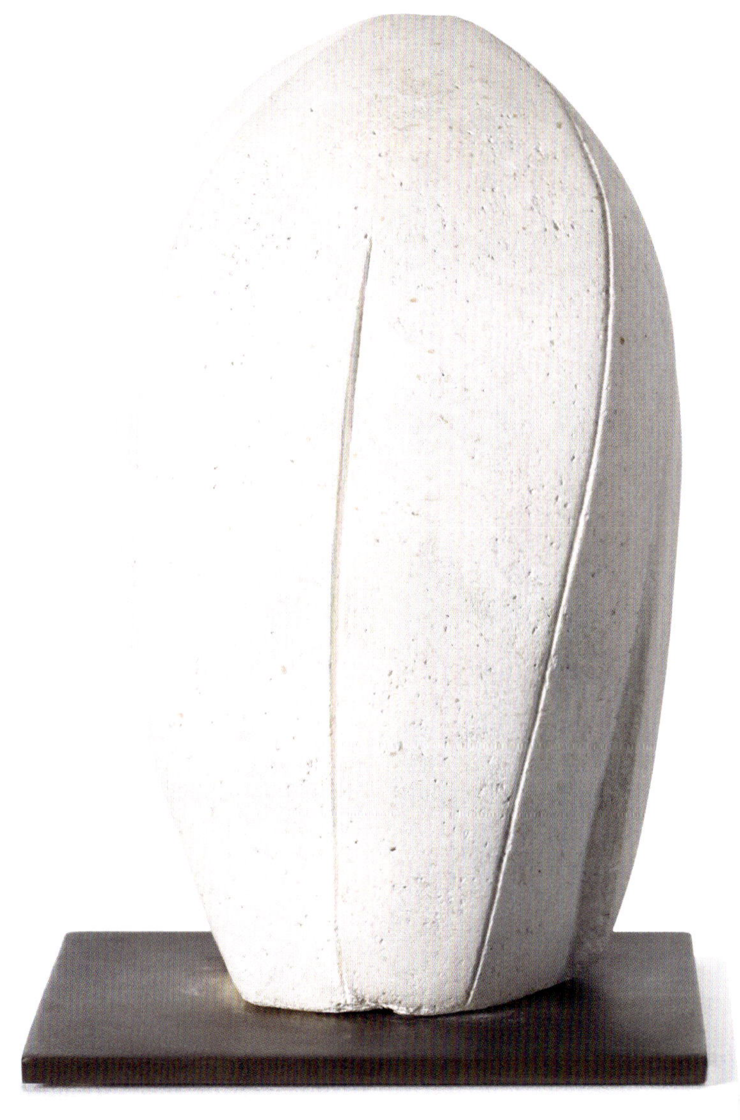

78 **Kudah**, 1989 marble, 103 × 44·5 × 28·8 cm (41 × 18 × 11 in) The Estate of Kim Lim

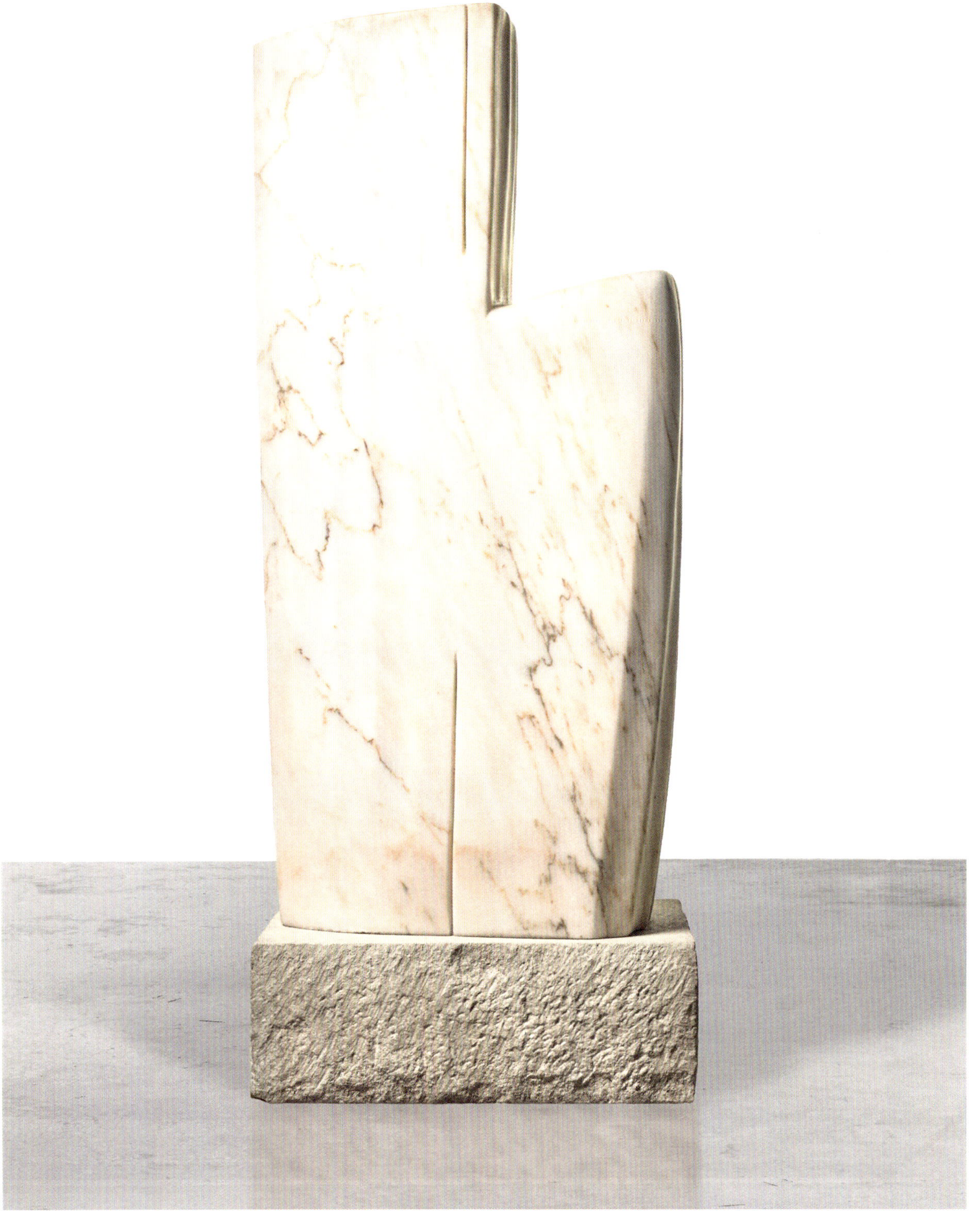

cancer in 1997. She kept the marble's surface not fully polished, with the base plinth rougher and more chiselled on its sides as if the abrading properties of the winds and waters of the island archipelago translated into deftly worked textures. Malay names and Malaysian locations also recur once more in this period, like *Kudah* (1989; fig.78), joining *Borneo II* (1964), and *Trengannu II* (1968; fig.79). But it is hard to tell whether these Malay titles held personal resonance with the artist. Lim asserts 'space as place', whereby the cultural positioning of the artwork is secondary to the physical placement of the work when on display.[10] Kim Lim once lamented that she did feel the isolation of not belonging, 'but it had the compensating element of freedom – a certain feeling of detachment from which one could view both East and West'.[11] Given that Lim lived through the British Colonial era and the horrors of the Japanese occupation in Malaya, what appears as both formal detachment and tentative attachment to biographical references in her work only goes to show the artist's humanity in her navigation of the complex terrains of reference points in art and life. As the artist wrote: 'I would like my work to be able to infer experiences beyond the piece itself. Infer rather than refer to something specific and particular.'[12]

Notes

1 Kim Lim, Interview with Cathy Courtney, London, 20 October 1995, *National Life Stories: Artists' Lives* (London: British Library, 1995), C466/51, transcript, p.94.
2 Lena Cheng, 'Sculptress who works in wood', *Her World* (December 1960), p.70.
3 Howard Rombough, 'Breaking the Rules: Kim Lim', *HOT*, undated, pp 38–40.
4 Kim Lim, artist notes, undated, the Kim Lim archive.
5 ibid., p.96.
6 I have written about Kim Lim's art in relation to her travel photographs in Joleen Loh, 'The Photographs of Kim Lim: A Visual Essay', *Art History*, vol.44, issue 3 (June 2021), special issue edited by Sonia Boyce and Dorothy Price, *Rethinking British Art: Black Artists and Modernism*, pp 532–52.
7 Kim Lim in Melanie Clulow, 'Carving a Niche', *Vogue* (July 1996), p.122.
8 Lim, *Artists' Lives*, p.99.
9 ibid., p.103.
10 Kim Lim, artist notes, undated, the Kim Lim archive.
11 ibid.
12 ibid.

79 **Trengannu II**, 1968 fibreglass, in four parts, each 39·4 × 66 × 78·7 cm (15 × 26 × 31 in) The Estate of Kim Lim

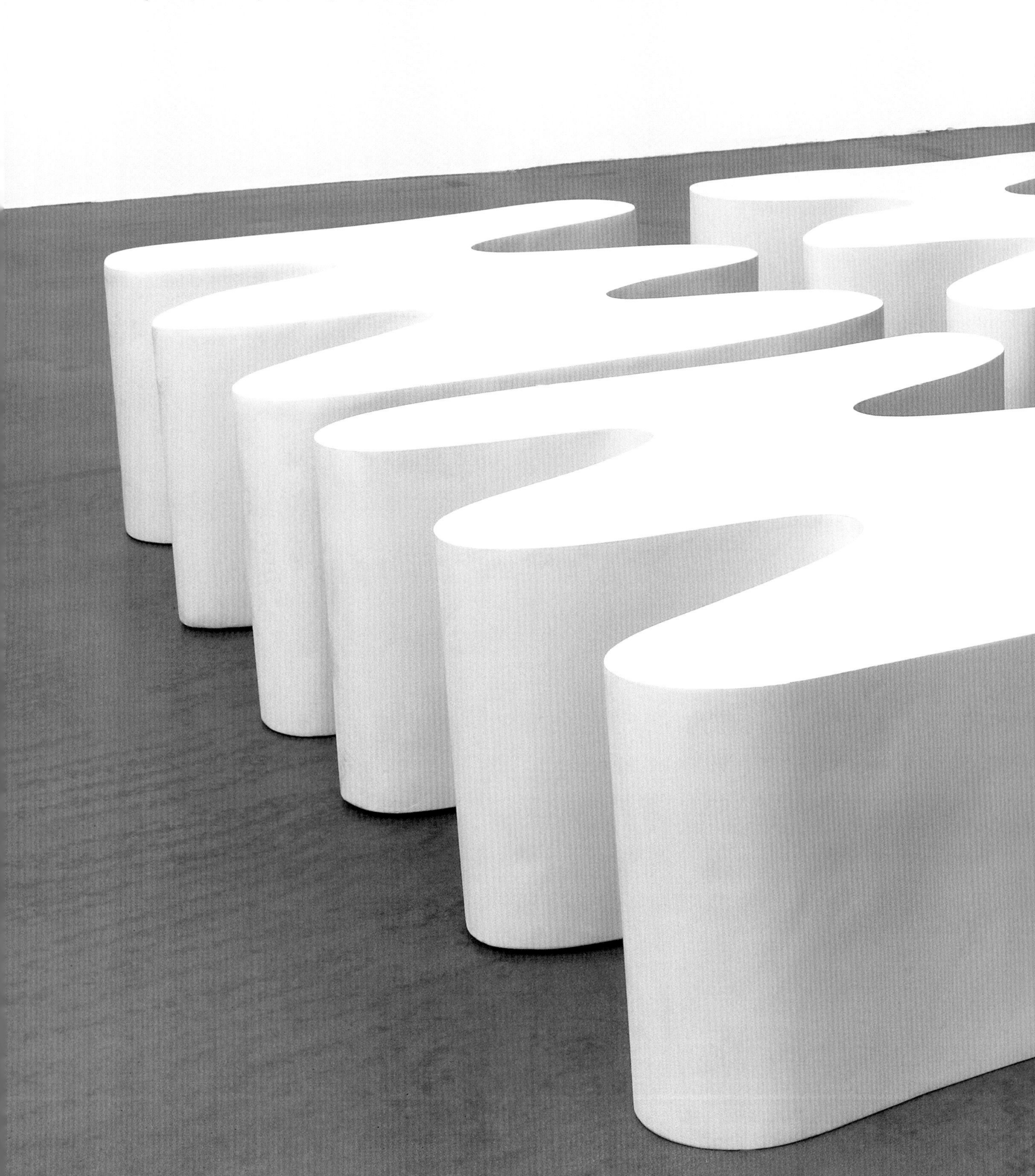

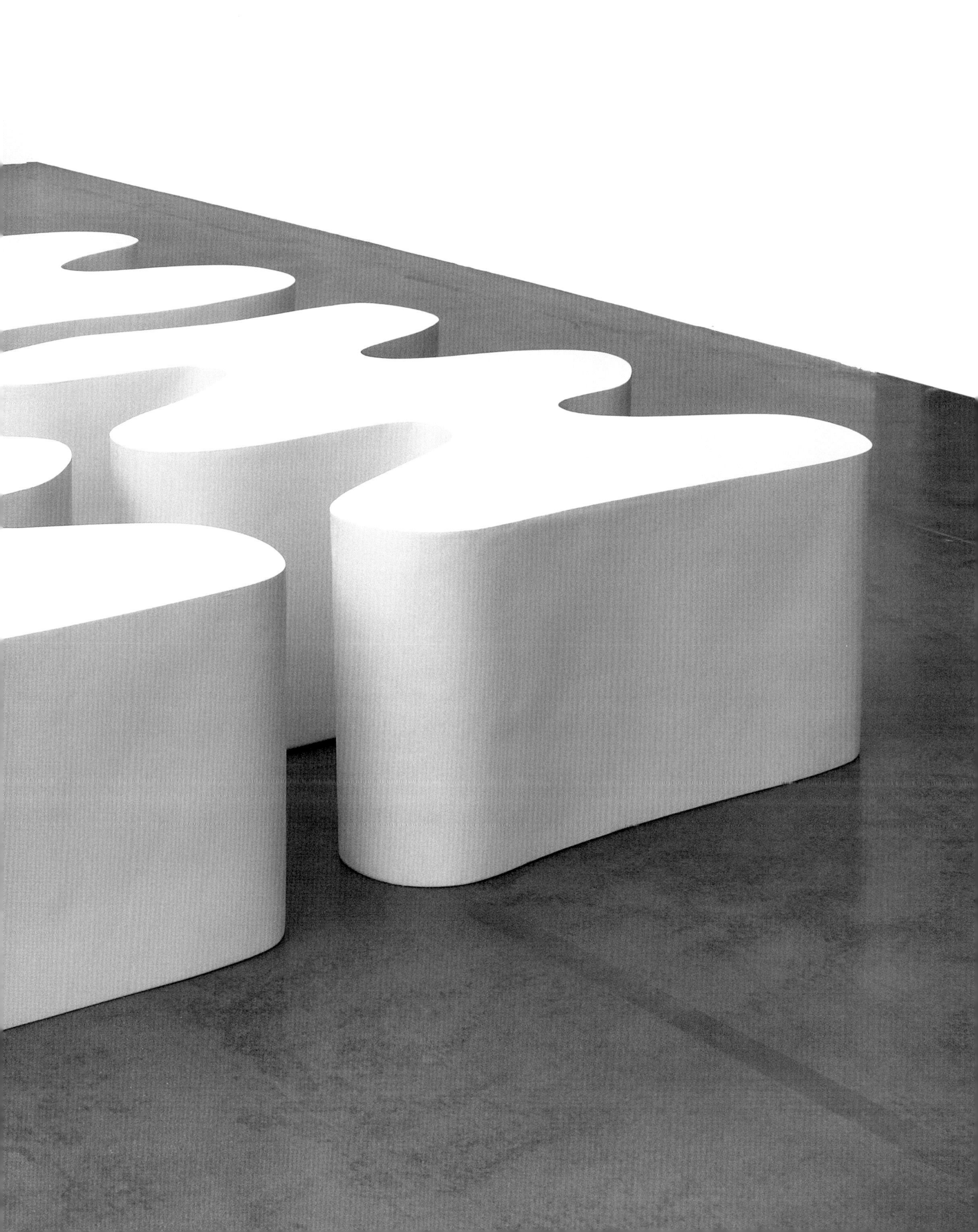

 Kim Lim at work in Camden Square The Estate of Kim Lim

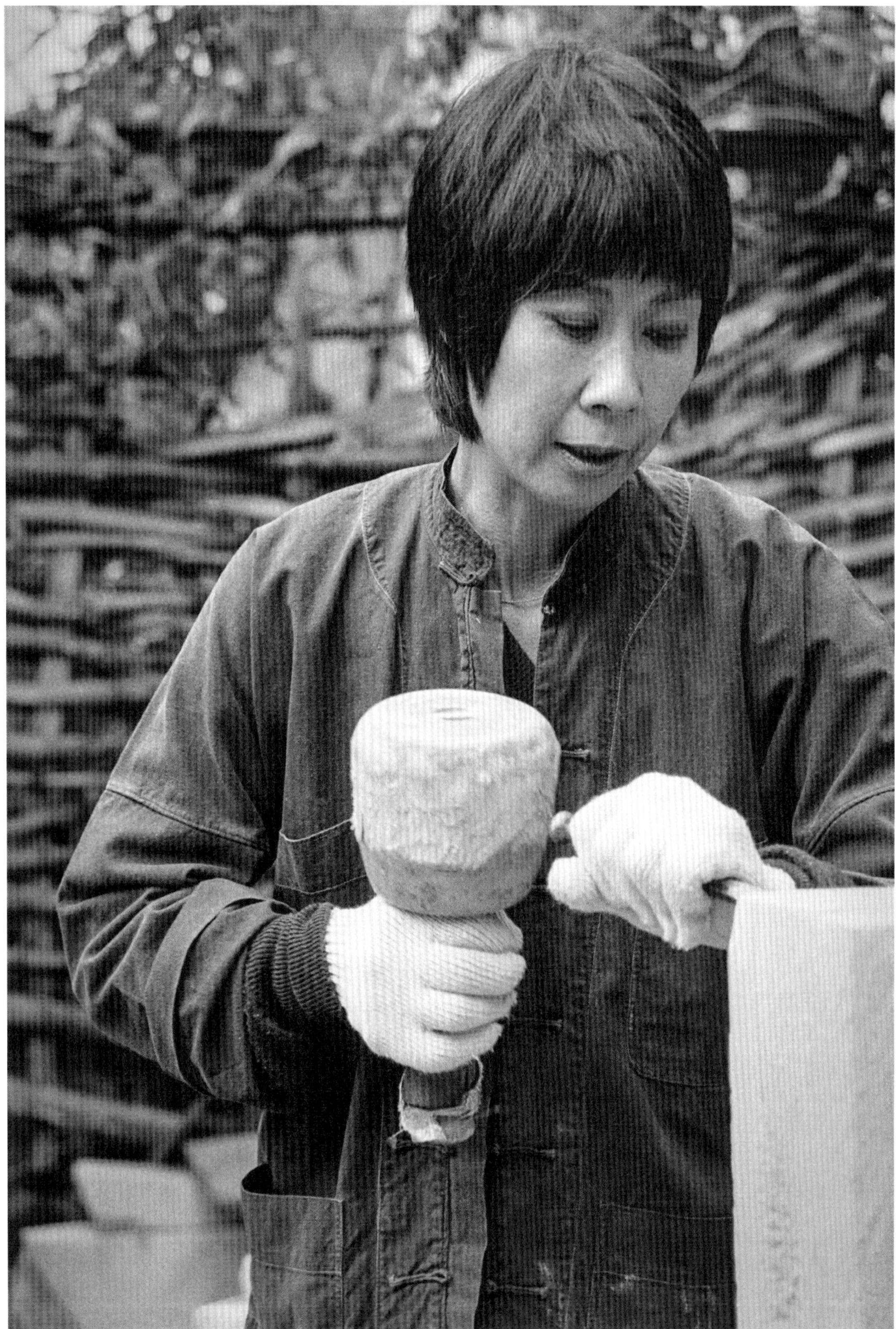

Bianca Chu

On Devotion: Some Questions on the Practice of an Estate

This chapter considers the work of the Estate of Kim Lim and its practice at the Turnbull Studio. The Turnbull Studio is the entity that functions as the custodian of the estates of the artists Kim Lim and William Turnbull. Today, it is the brainchild of Alex and Johnny Turnbull, the sons of the artists, supported by me, as strategic advisor and representative. I suggest in this text that the work of an estate is fundamentally a creative practice – the Turnbull Studio serves as the nexus for the legacies of Kim Lim and William Turnbull, where a web of relationships, experiences, memories, knowledge bases, actions, objects and materials converge. In describing some of the recent ethical and practical activities of the studio, I consider some aspects of our work which are informal, discursive, subtle and often invisible.[1]

Echo(es)

The work of an estate is to constantly (re)tread and (re)trace old ground and this work is paradoxically situated and in constant motion. It operates primarily in the fields of art and art history, and yet tackles economies and markets, anthropological and social praxis, as well as the internal work of emotional labour. Reverberating throughout are echoes of the past: histories that have been obscured, that resist simple digestion and assimilation into dominant (art) historical narratives and thus require acts of storytelling. Furthermore, this work is memory-work that is deeply private – an excavation that is temporally never located in the past because the work is about engaging with the present and potential *futurities* of the past. Therefore, an estate's work has to contend with living histories that affect current states of mind and cultures, and through their polyphony, we are gifted the possibility to intervene with fresh stories and break new ground.

When Alex, Johnny and I visited Penang, Malaysia, in spring 2023, our trip brought us back to their ancestral 'home', where Kim Lim had lived as a child – a journey that I too recently experienced in December 2022, returning to Taiwan where my parents were born for the first time since the pandemic.

81 **Day**, 1966 on the podium roof of the MSA building, Singapore, undated The Estate of Kim Lim

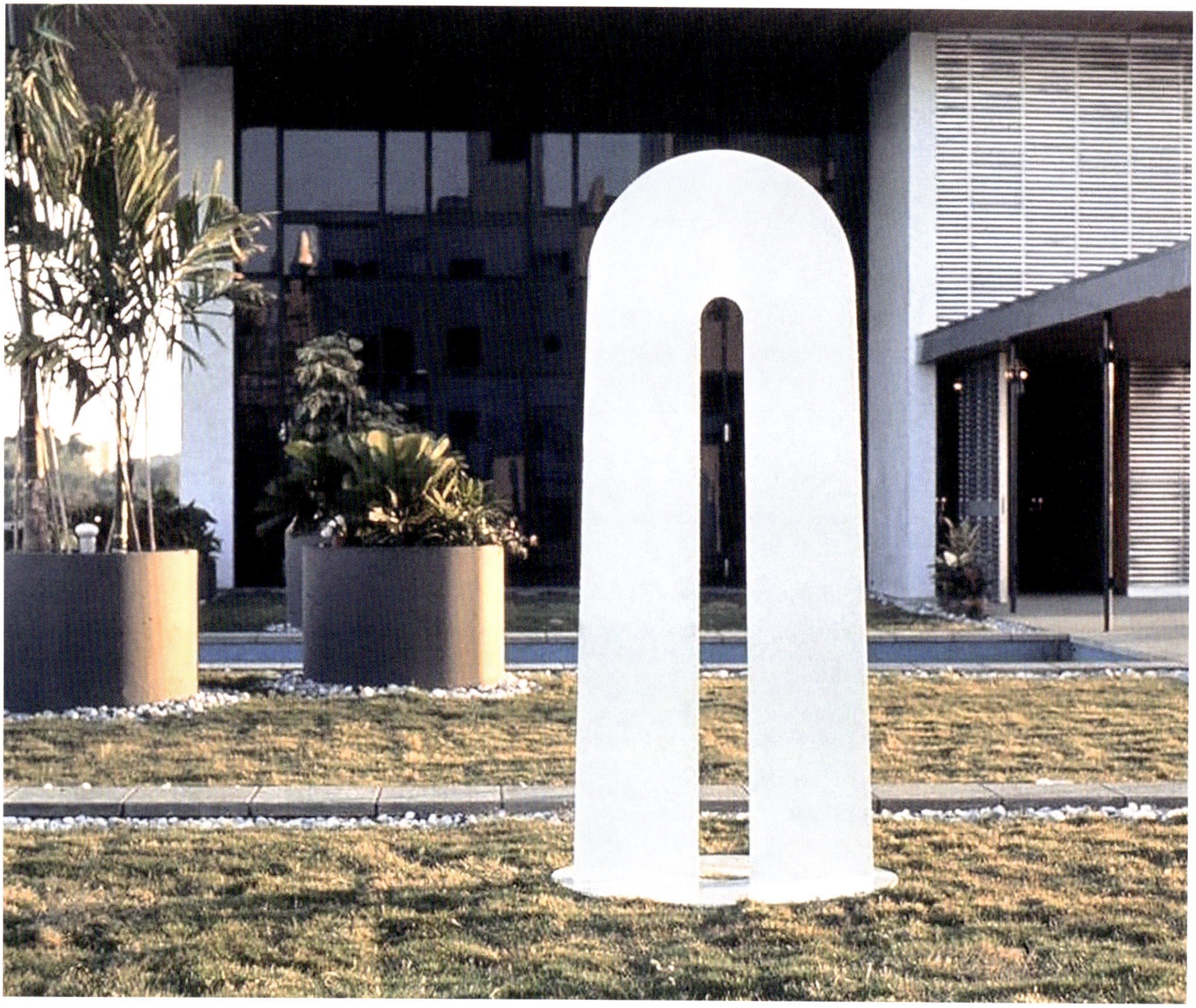

In Penang, we visited and interviewed Datuk Lim Chong Keat, a 93-year-old 'polymath and pioneering architect'[2] and close friend of Buckminster Fuller, who knew Kim Lim and William Turnbull through his own family connections with 'Kim's family' in Singapore.[3] He relayed that, for his second major architectural project in Singapore, he designed the MSA (Malaysia-Singapore Airlines) building.[4] Keen to showcase local artists whose practices he felt resonated with his own modernist concerns, he commissioned Lim's sculpture *Day* (1966; fig.81) which became her first public art commission and one of the rare sculptures by her that can live outside.[5]

Alex and Johnny first went with their parents to Penang in the early seventies, in what Alex recounted as 'the place where it [kind of] all began'.[6] Though Lim was born in Singapore (prior to independence), her earliest memories are from growing up in Penang and Malacca. She recalls how her parents had to navigate 'dealing with colonial Europeans [in Penang] who were wondering what the Chinese family was doing there'.[7] Here, her father, magistrate Lim Koon Teck, voluntarily stayed to mediate when the British abandoned the territory in the face of the impending Japanese invasion and occupation from 1941 to 1945.[8] Lim remembers this 'saved [their] lives' because the Japanese forces found her father 'useful' since he spoke the local language and had 'respect' for the population.[9]

Nearly eighty years later, a chance encounter in Penang revealed new information. At the Bellevue The Penang Hill Hotel, owned by Lim Chong Keat, with unparalleled views of the city and mainland, we saw the historic map 'A Map of the Malay Peninsula, 1906' which contained the name 'Trengannu' – a title Lim gave to a series of works made between 1967 and 1968 with a distinctive 'wave' form (fig.79) also seen in prints made shortly thereafter in 1969 (fig.83). For a long time, we had considered *Trengannu* to be a misspelling. Today, there is only Terengganu province in Malaysia but, back in 1906, Trengannu was its romanised spelling. Lim, in all her meticulous attention to detail had not made some haphazard typo. 'Trengannu' left an echo in her imagination – a small but illuminating example of how memory, even the kind that is wholly private and individual, is continuously reaching backwards (or forwards) in the present practice of an estate.

82 **Echo**, 1967 stainless steel, enamel paint and zinc coating, 77 × 80 × 80 cm (30 × 31 × 31 in) Collection of National Gallery Singapore

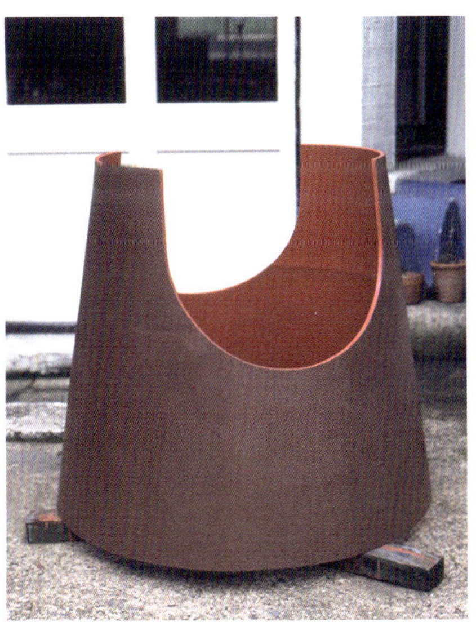

The 'Unstruck' Sculpture

Echo (fig.82) is a 1967 work by Kim Lim now in the collection of the National Gallery Singapore. The title references the repetitive reverberation of a sonic wave. Sound is not often thought of as inherent to sculpture – or rather sculptures, particularly those made of more 'classical' materials, are not often perceived as possessing an intrinsic sonic quality. We may ascribe material qualities such as density, weight, balance, volume, malleability or porosity to wood, marble, stone and bronze, but how often do we consider a sculpture's silence, or its apparent silence? Beyond the material presence of a finished sculpture, which is the object that we most readily engage with, in the context of 'art world(s)', might we contemplate (and speculate) on the sculptural practice of Kim Lim from a perspective of vibration, sound and energy so as to consider what might be spiritual in her practice, as well the legacy of her work today?

83 **'Free Forms'**, 1969 etching on paper, 53 × 51 cm (21 × 20 in) The Estate of Kim Lim

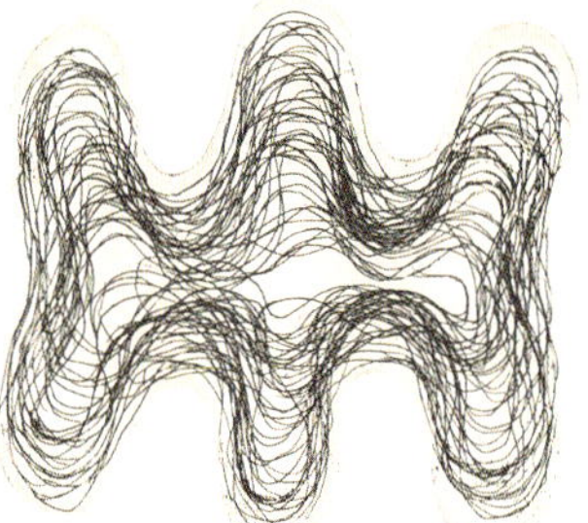

Alex and Johnny have often recounted the determination of their mother's character. For example, after an invasive spinal surgery in 1990, Lim carved the largest stone sculpture she had ever produced. Carving and reducing seemed to be acts of faith that formed the basis of her creative and spiritual practice. Here, 'spiritual practice' may be thought of as a series of actions that embody one's creative lifeforce – or *prana*, also defined as vital energy in the Vedic traditions. Energy is neither created nor destroyed, according to the first law of thermodynamics, and, therefore, is unbound by space or time.

In an interview in 1995 Lim noted she had been 'doing a lot of yoga and reading a lot of Indian philosophy'.[10] Her sons told me once that she was a practitioner of Iyengar yoga. Lim was an explorer of a wide range of philosophies, well-acquainted with Buddhism and Daoism, whose folk traditions and rituals she experienced directly 'by osmosis' during her childhood.[11] By her own admission, she was interested in the Vedic and Yogic traditions, as a corporeal, spiritual and intellectual pursuit.[12] She expressed once to her interviewer:

> I would like to believe that there's something a little bit outside just the humanity that is more powerful, but it has to be an energy, it's not a person or a thing ... I'd like to think that there's a benign energy somewhere ... A dear friend of mine told me that energy never dies, it's only changed, so, if I am a person made of atoms, and it goes away, it doesn't, I suppose it just changes.[13]

Here, she suggests a belief in the existence of a flow of energy that permeates all things. Arguably, this energy is, therefore, immanent in any artistic practice, as it resides in the (artistic) soul and (artful) actions. It is also said that sound is the 'essence of all energy'.[14] By this logic, anything produced or created with such an intention or belief may be considered to possess its own vibration, its own sound. Could the apparent silence of a sculpture in fact give way to a new experience of it through sound? Kim once described the 'sensuousness of wood blocks', and the 'sounds they make', recalling how as a child she witnessed in local markets 'when people sold things, they would clack things together, like bamboo or two bits of wood, and you would know by the sound of the clack'.[15] Johnny recalled the sound of his mother chiselling as 'tac, tac, tac' (fig.80).[16]

The discernment of sounds is important. In the practice of Nāda yoga, described in the *Hatha Yoga Pradipika* – the 14th-century classical Sanskrit manual compiled by Nath Yogi Swatmarama – a path to *samadhi* (enlightenment) is possible through deep inner listening, culminating in the ability to hear *anāhata nāda*, 'the unstruck sound',[17] or what Sharon Gannon calls 'soundless sound which dissolves all other sound'.[18] The manual distinguishes between 'subtle sound [which] is not caused by two things being struck together, whereas gross sound can only occur by two objects coming together. Subtle sound is heard by the consciousness itself. Gross sound is heard through the ear sending vibrations to the brain.'[19] To reach an awareness of this imperceptible sound, the practitioner must cultivate an advanced skill of listening which is distinct from hearing because it attunes to a sound different from the mere intake of the ambient sound around us all the time. One method to cultivate good listening, Gannon explains, is to 'appreciate good music'.[20]

If we acknowledge the power of music to enliven our hearing sense and support deep listening through the synthesis of rhythm, pitch, duration, tempo and melody, then we might also consider how the body acts as a multi-sensory instrument through which we interface with external and internal worlds. I like to think of Kim Lim in her studio performing a symphonic exercise during the act of reducing and carving her raw material, and that, today, we engage with the subtler vibrations that percolate through her works.

Diving deeper, music is also not only comprised of 'positive' elements, it is said that 'music without pause is white noise', so the silence in *the space between* notes remains fundamental for the blissful evocation of harmonic sound.[21] Furthermore, the spaces between notes, are in, Nāda yoga terms, 'subtle' sounds. By coincidence, *The Space Between* is the title of a 2019 musical composition by Johnny Turnbull and Tom Heslop.[22] Johnny has recalled how he learned of the concise word for this concept of an intervening space: an interstice.

Interstices is the title of a series of sculptures by Kim Lim from the 1970s, including the iteration *Interstices II* (1977; fig.84). Involving four linear, carved wooden beams, each with different intervening empty spaces in its centre, *Interstices I* and *II* have been presented in various configurations: in a corner, on the floor, against a wall (figs 84 and 85). At the centre of each slat are rectangular openings – the sculpture itself is comprised of interstices, and its very presence implies an interstice.

Illustrating these simultaneous and yet anachronistic threads invites a different kind of encounter with sculptures by Lim that is both visual and material in its presence. It allows us to listen, receive and imagine their harmonious, consonant energetic field and vibrational frequency. The silence of a sculpture isn't perhaps as much an absence of sound as it is an indication of the presence of imperceptible sound. A process that may be concurrently subtle and generous remains of great interest to our practice at the Turnbull Studio and links back to the approach that lies at the heart of the work of the Estate.

84 **Interstices II**, 1977 mahogany, in four parts, each 289·5 cm (114 in) in height The Estate of Kim Lim

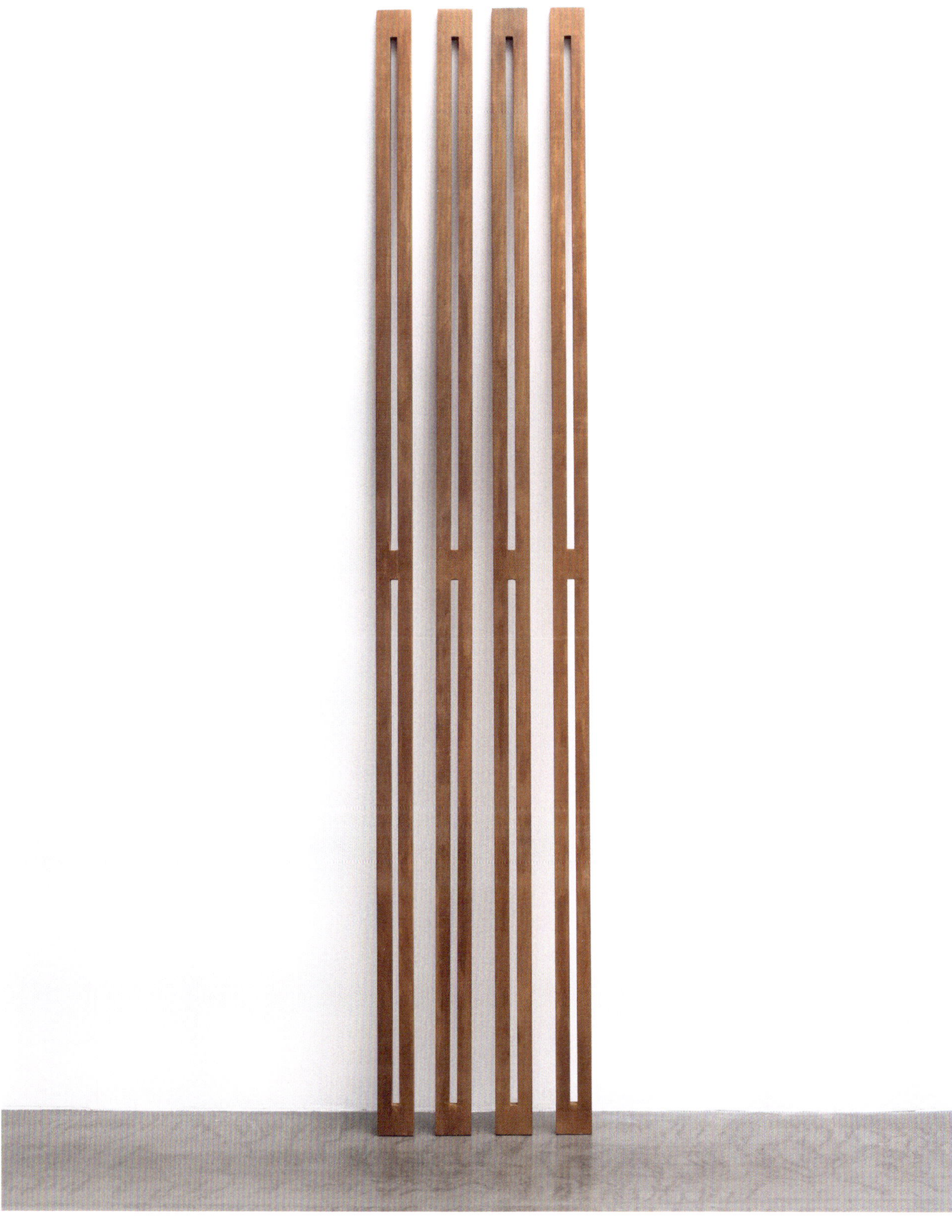

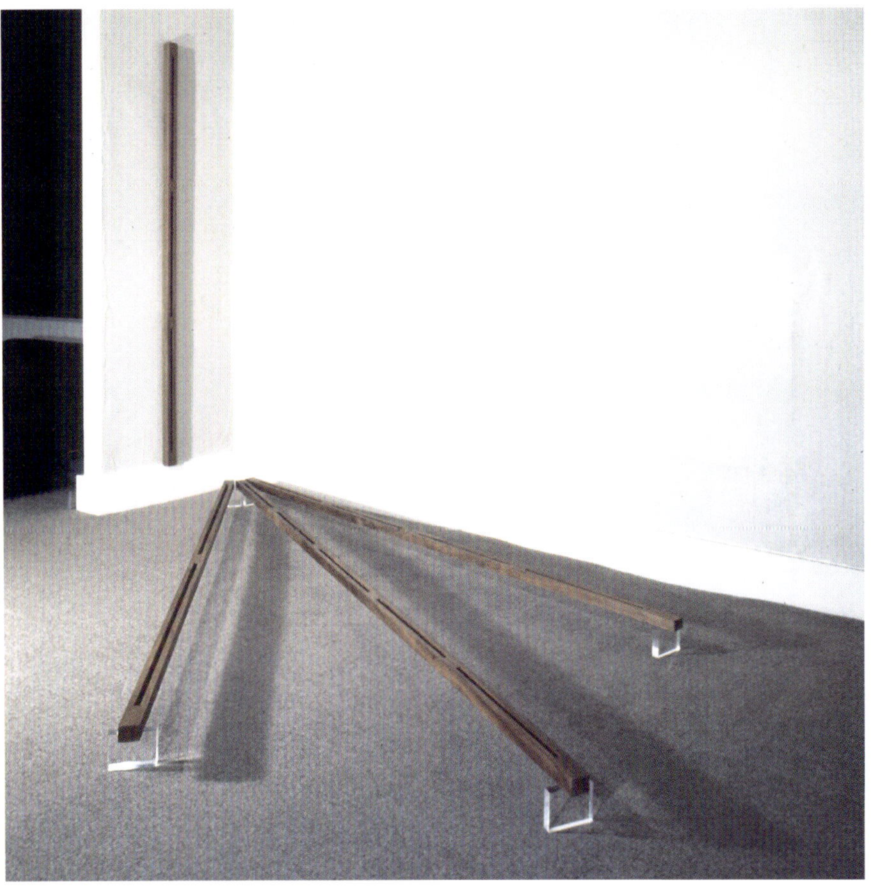

On Devotion

I consider the bedrock of the Turnbull Studio to be an ethical paradigm premised on devotion – specifically, that a devotional *practice* informs the creative, operational and strategic outputs that have come to define our understanding of the work. For us, devotion invokes the polyphonic sensation of the union of discipline, belief, love and integrity within the body. As such, the work is embodied in our individual and shared memories, experiences, expressions and knowledge bases. It must necessarily be intuitive *and* empirical, felt and directly evidenced, and led by our translations of the enduring traces of Kim Lim (fig.86). A devotional practice is unique to each person and, in the case of estates – unique as they are – there is no template for their work.

For a long time, Estates have been perceived as homogenous to some extent: a 'productive' approach by the remaining family members of a respected artist might naturally seek the 'best' gallery (for them) at a given

86 Kim Lim's studio, Camden Square, London, mid-1960s The Estate of Kim Lim

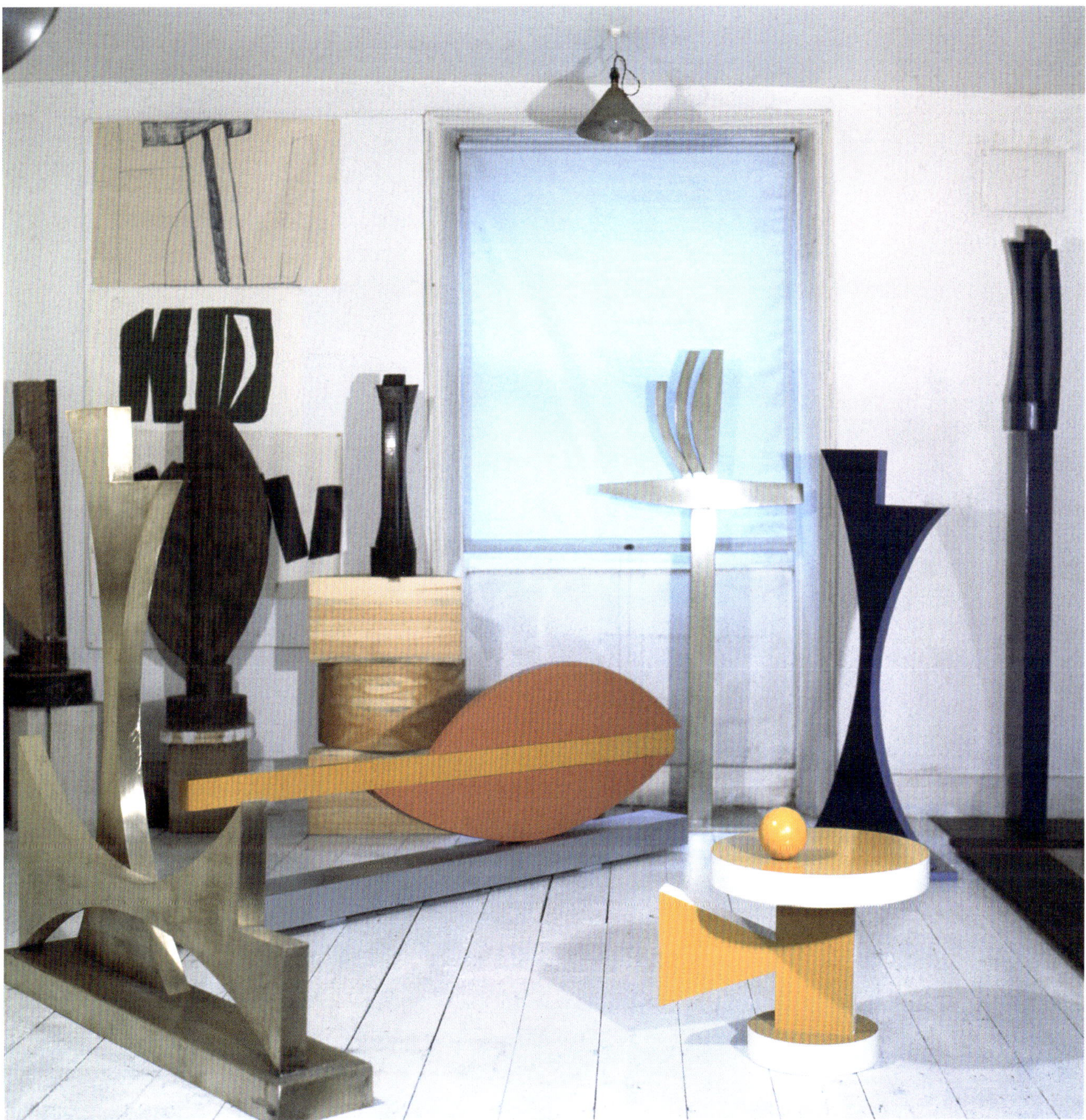

moment in time to support and prolong the lifespan of that artist's work. This might involve a more laissez-faire attitude towards who buys or supports the work and who shows the artist. An estate might even be lucky enough to form a foundation one day that performs and serves beyond two generations after an artist passes away. The question of whether new methodologies and structures for artist estates might be afforded space in our current globalised, interdependent, cosmopolitan societies and disrupt existing models is, in my view, an urgent one. The Kim Lim Estate reflects and contends with many cultural landscapes and complex systems: institutional, commercial, academic, conceptions of 'regional' or 'local' versus 'international', 'Asia' (as opposed to 'the West'), diaspora, gender and race – to name a few terms which are themselves problematic.

In response, we practise with varying degrees of conscious, rigorous diligence – planning, interpreting, archiving, corresponding, researching, lovingly caring, objectifying, protecting and entrusting – coupled with a strong dose of nerve, belief and grit. Some of the less visible actions that come to mind range from the very practical, such as the labour-intensive management of inventory and digital image banks, to the exceptionally sensitive, such as choosing what kind of partners and collaborators to work with and discerning their motivations. As such, devotional practice here is *effort*. In carrying out an immense labour (of love), how best then to move from the invisible space and realm of an Estate to interface with the outside 'world'?

An estate is the custodian of a life's work and, therefore, should also defer to what is known about such a life, as much as it is its job to unearth and shed light on that which might be obscured, *and* to support fresh readings and contexts. For example, Lim's polite refusal to participate in the 1989 exhibition *The Other Story*: *Afro-Asian Artists in Post-war Britain* due to not wanting to 'other herself' highlighted something that she rejected, but nevertheless had to navigate.[23] Therefore, as the international art industry continues to move towards transnational decolonising approaches, and issues around representation swing from necessary interventions to the dangerous trappings of self-marginalisation and tokenism, the estate must discern and choose within which spheres to operate.

In the same way that living artists and creators now are re-negotiating the terms of engagement with the external worlds of collectors, audiences, commercial and institutional structures, and even virtual worlds, should an artist's estate also reconsider its relationships to these players and their worlds? Who would best devote their time, energy, care and empathy to the life and practice of an artist who is no longer present to decide? Therefore, when it comes to devotion, we must ask what it means in different contexts. For example, estates must discern how their work engages in public and private realms. 'Publics' are not only the collections of museums, which can display and conserve artworks, but the forums and space created by people both from within and outside the art milieu. An estate must also interact with the art market(s) through commercial galleries, auction houses, art advisors and fairs, which can be tricky due to the entanglement of social, cultural and financial capital. Whilst any estate requires operational funding, it also requires collectors and collaborators who are willing to empathise with its ethos, temporality, pace and needs. What is devotion in this context? It could be taking a path of non-action, it might be waiting and seeing, it might also be actively defending and protecting. It is, importantly, cultivating relationships with a diverse range of talent – individuals and groups who are willing to support the work emotionally, structurally, financially; we are grateful to have met some of these people in our work.

In the end, a devotional practice is the willingness and desire to engage with difficult, even contradictory, ideas, questions, situations and relationships, and their impact on the legacy of an artist and the lifespan of an estate. It is a *known unknown* how any culture or history might remember and respond to such a legacy. Therefore, an estate can empower those who support its work and be empowered by the supporters in return. A devotional practice, then, remains an act of faith that the actions (and non-actions) performed are the precise ones that are needed at a moment in time, played out at the rhythm and tempo demanded.

Notes

1 This text was compiled through personal reflection, observation and conversation, and was written whilst on the road with Alex and Johnny Turnbull in Hong Kong, Penang, Seoul and Gwangju between 19 March and 8 April 2023.
2 *Session 0: Lim Chong Keat*, 17 November 2019, lecture at National Gallery Singapore, excerpt, https://www.nationalgallery.sg/sites/default/files/Session-0-Lim-Chong-Keat-Print-02.pdf, p.1.
3 Lim Chong Keat, correspondence with the author, 26 April 2023.
4 Conversation between Alex and Johnny Turnbull and Lim Chong Keat at which the author was also present, Penang, 26 March 2023.
5 Another version of *Day* is in the collection of The Hepworth Wakefield (fig.1).
6 Alex Turnbull in conversation with the author, Penang, 26 March 2023.
7 Kim Lim, Interview with Cathy Courtney, London, 20 October 1995, *National Life Stories: Artists' Lives* (London: British Library, 1995), C466/51, transcript, p.34.
8 ibid., p.33.
9 ibid., pp 44–5.
10 ibid., p.28.
11 ibid., p.10.
12 ibid., p.10.
13 ibid., p.27.
14 Sharon Gannon, 'Nadam: Listening for the Unstruck Sound', *Jivamukti Yoga* (June 2003), https://jivamuktiyoga.com/fotm/nadam-listening-unstruck-sound/.
15 Lim, *Artists' Lives*, p.62.
16 Johnny Turnbull in conversation with the author, 3 April 2023.
17 *Hatha Yoga Pradipika*: *Light on Hatha Yoga*, [1985] 2014, commentary by Swami Muktibodhananda, under the guidance of Swami Satyananda Saraswati, Munger, India: Yoga Publications Trust.
18 Gannon, 'Nadam: Listening for the Unstruck Sound'.
19 *Hatha Yoga Pradipika*, p.558.
20 Gannon, 'Nadam: Listening for the Unstruck Sound'.
21 Andrew Smith of Blue Rose Astrology in conversation with the author, 19 October 2022.
22 https://soundcloud.com/roninproductions/the-space-between/s-TXd3P70CYu4.
23 For more on this event, see Wenny Teo's text in this publication.

87 Kim Lim working on **Twice** (1966) in 1968 The Estate of Kim Lim

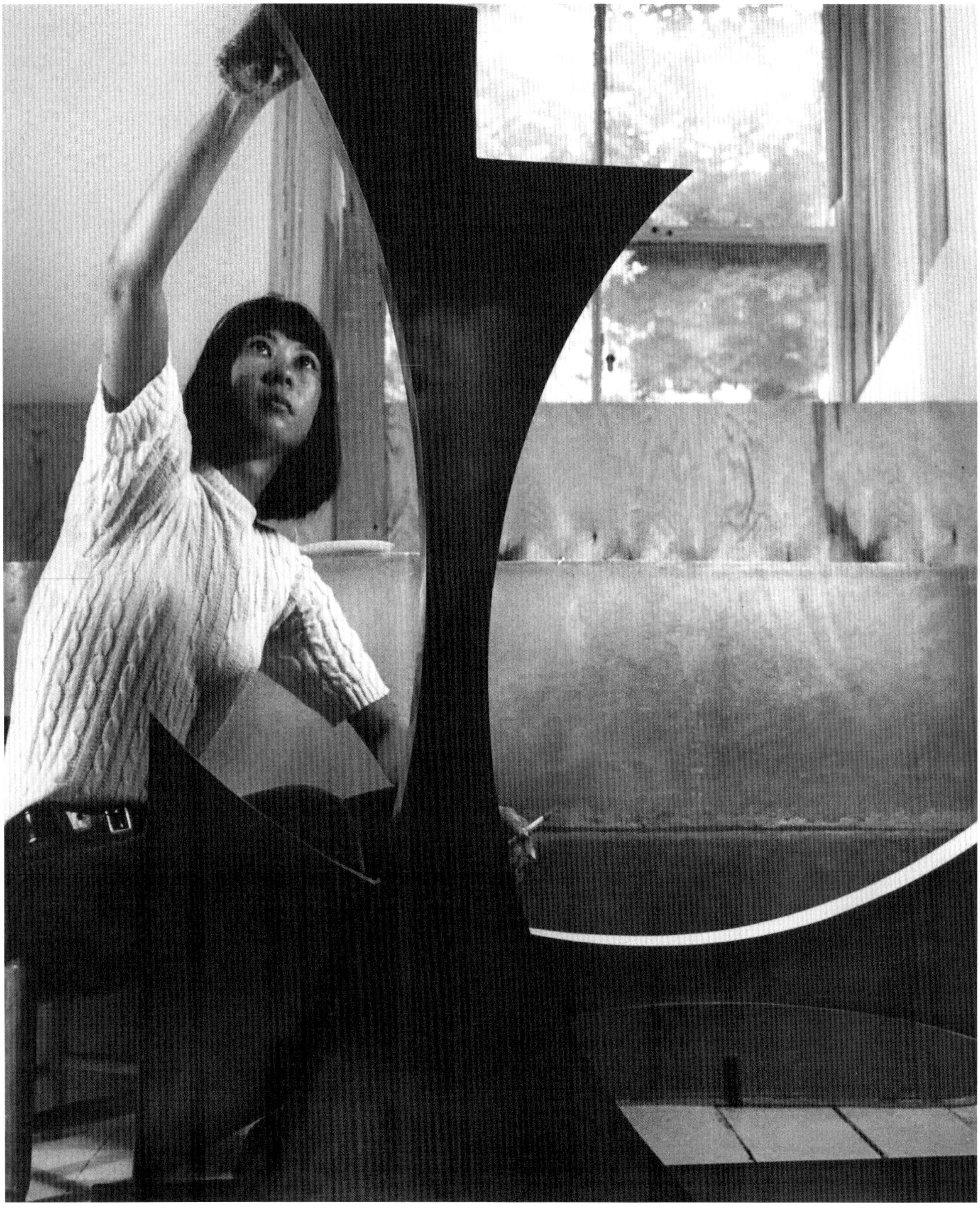

Chronology

1936 Kim Lim is born in Singapore. She spends her childhood in Malaysia, specifically in Penang and Malacca, until she moves back to Singapore to finish her schooling.

1954 Lim moves to London to study at St Martin's School of Art. She trains for a brief period of time under sculptors Elisabeth Frink and Anthony Caro.

1956 Lim transfers to the Slade School of Fine Art where she studies printmaking with Anthony Gross and Stanley Jones and continues working in sculpture.

1957 Lim meets artist William Turnbull in a ceramics workshop led by ceramicist Helen Hatori.

1960 Lim graduates from the Slade and obtains her own studio in a disused chemistry laboratory in West Hampstead. Lim marries Turnbull.

1961 Lim takes part in her first group show, *26 Young Sculptors* at the The Institute of Contemporary Arts in London. Lim and Turnbull move into 40 Camden Square, where they live and each have their own studio.

1962 *Samurai* (1961) is acquired for the Arts Council Collection. It is the first work by Lim to be acquired by a public institution or gallery. Lim's first child, Alex, is born.

1963 Lim's second child, Johnny, is born.

1966 Lim has her first solo exhibition, at Axiom Gallery in London. The architect Lim Chong Keat commissions *Day*. One version of the work is displayed atop the Malaysia-Singapore Airlines building, and another at *Sculpture in the Open Air* in Battersea Park, London. It is her first work displayed outdoors.

1974 Lim has her first solo show in Singapore, at Alpha Gallery.

1976 The Tate Gallery acquires almost 30 works by Lim, particularly prints and works on paper made between 1960 and 1972.

1977 Lim is included in the Hayward Annual exhibition. She is the only woman and artist of the Global Majority in the exhibition.

1978 For the second Hayward Annual, Kim Lim is part of the first all-female selection committee along with Tess Jaray, Liliane Lijn, Gillian Wise Ciobotaru and Rita Donagh. They select mostly women to exhibit.

1979 Kim Lim has her first major retrospective exhibition, at The Roundhouse Gallery in London. After this exhibition, Lim begins to work in stone.

1982 Lim's stone works go on display for the first time at Nicola Jacobs Gallery, London.

1984 Lim and Turnbull display recent sculptures, drawings and prints at the National Museum Art Gallery in Singapore. The same year, they travel to China together.

1993 The first version of *Riverstone* (1990–91), Lim's largest work, is displayed at Roche Court Sculpture Park alongside her other stone sculptures. Lim embarked on these physically demanding pieces after undergoing spinal surgery and while later suffering from cancer.

1997 Kim Lim dies from cancer in London. A memorial tribute is added near her sculpture *Sea-Stone* (1989), then on display in Tate's Duveen Galleries.

1999 In development before Lim's death, a survey exhibition of Lim's later work is held at Camden Art Centre, London

Public Collections

Arts Council Collection, Southbank Centre, London, UK
Atkinson Art Gallery, Southport, UK
British Council Collection, UK
British Museum, London, UK
Fukuyama City Museum, Hiroshima, Japan
Government Art Collection, London, UK
Guggenheim Abu Dhabi, UAE
Ingram Collection, UK
Jerwood Collection, UK
Leicestershire Education Council, UK
Middelheim Museum, Belgium
M+ Museum, Hong Kong
National Gallery Singapore, Singapore
Nagaoka Museum of Modern Art, Japan
Pallant House Gallery, Chichester, UK
Palm Springs Art Museum, Palm Springs, US
National Galleries Scotland, Edinburgh, UK
Sheffield Museums, Sheffield, UK
Southampton City Art Gallery, Southampton, UK
Tate, UK
Wakefield Council Permanent Art Collection (The Hepworth Wakefield), Wakefield, UK

Solo Exhibitions

1966 *Kim Lim*, Axiom Gallery, London
1968 *Kim Lim*, Axiom Gallery, London
1973 *Kim Lim: Prints*, Waddington Galleries, London
1974 *Kim Lim*, Alpha Gallery, Singapore
1975 *Kim Lim: Prints*, Museum of Modern Art, Oxford
Kim Lim, Felicity Samuel Gallery, London
1977 *Kim Lim: Graphics*, Tate Gallery, London
1979 *Kim Lim: Sculpture, Drawings, Prints*, The Roundhouse Gallery, London
1981 *Kim Lim*, Southampton Museum and Art Gallery, Southampton
1982 *Kim Lim*, Nicola Jacobs Gallery, London
1983 *Kim Lim*, Arcade Gallery, Harrogate
1984 *Kim Lim: Prints and Drawings, 1972–80*, Nicola Jacobs Gallery, London
Kim Lim, National Museum and Art Gallery, Singapore
1985 *Kim Lim*, Nicola Jacobs Gallery, London
1990 *Kim Lim*, Waddington Galleries, London
1993 *Orangery Show*, Roche Court, New Art Centre, Wiltshire
Kim Lim, Flowers East, London
1995 *Kim Lim: Sculpture and Works on Paper*, Yorkshire Sculpture Park, Wakefield
1999 *Kim Lim*, Camden Arts Centre, London, toured to Mead Art Gallery, Warwick Arts Centre
Kim Lim: A Tribute Exhibition, Singapore Art Museum, Singapore
2014 *Kim Lim: Carvings*, New Art Centre, Roche Court, Salisbury
2015 *Conversations with Stone Paper*, Asia House Gallery, London
2017 *Kim Lim*, Sl2 Gallery, London
2018 *Kim Lim: Sculpting Light*, STPI Gallery, Singapore
Kim Lim, Sl2 Gallery, London
2020 *Kim Lim: Carving and Printing*, Tate Britain, London
2023 *Kim Lim: Space, Rhythm & Light*, The Hepworth Wakefield, Wakefield
2024 *Kim Lim*, National Gallery Singapore, Singapore.

Selected Group Exhibitions

1961 *26 Young Sculptors*, ICA, London
Deuxième Biennale de Paris, Paris
1962 *Sculpture Today & Tomorrow*, Bear Lane Gallery, Oxford
3rd International Biennale of Prints, Tokyo
1966 *Sculpture in the Open Air*, Battersea Park, London
Chromatic Sculpture, Arts Council Gallery, Cambridge
25 Camden Artists, Camden Central Library, London
1967 *Expo '67*, British Pavilion, Montreal
Transatlantic Graphics, Camden Arts Centre, London
Leicestershire Collection, Whitechapel Art Gallery, London
Nagaoka Prize Exhibition, Nagaoka Museum, Japan
Sculpture 1960–67 from the Arts Council Collection, Cumberland House Museum, Portsmouth, travelling to Worcester; Leeds; Swindon; Hull; Walsall; Oldham; Plymouth; Leamington; Accrington; King's Lynn; Lincoln; Stafford; Bolton; Doncaster; Sunderland; St Ives; Southampton; Stockport; Kidderminster; Mansfield; Derby; Birkenhead; Falmouth; Folkestone; Cheltenham; Norwich; Reading; Brighton; Lincoln; Southend
1968 *Sculpture in a City*, Arts Council exhibition. Touring exhibition: Post & Mail Building, Birmingham; Goree Piazza, Liverpool; Southampton Civic Centre
Summer Exhibition, Museum of Modern Art, Oxford
Prospect '68, Dusseldorf
Mostra Mercato d'Arte Contemporanea, Florence
1969 *Open Air Sculpture*, Middelheim, Antwerp
1970 *British Sculpture out of the Sixties*, ICA, London
3me Salon Internationale de Galeries Pilotes, Musée cantonal des Beaux-Arts, and Musée d'Art Moderne de la Ville de Paris, Paris
1974 *Rottweil Festival*, Rottweil, Germany
1975 *Print Biennale*, Ljubljana, Yugoslavia
1976 *Inaugural Exhibition*, National Museum Art Gallery, Singapore
Cast. Modelled. Constructed: Three Aspects of British 20th Century Art, Tate Gallery, London
1977 *Hayward Annual*, Hayward Gallery, London
1979 *International Biennale of Prints*, Tokyo
69th British International Print Biennale, Bradford
Biennale of European Graphic Art, Heidelberg, Germany
The First Exhibition, Nicola Jacobs Gallery, London
1980 *Norwegian International Print Biennale*, Fredrikstad Library, Norway
Sculpture, Nicola Jacobs Gallery, London
1981 *Print Biennale*, Ljubljana, Yugoslavia
Summer Exhibition, Nicola Jacobs Gallery, London
Camden Artists, Camden Arts Centre, London
Sculpture for the Blind, Tate Gallery, London
1982 *Women's Art Show 1550–1950*, Nottingham Castle Museum, Nottingham
British Sculpture 1951–1980, Whitechapel Art Gallery, London
1984 *Group Show*, Yorkshire Sculpture Park
Contemporary Carving, Plymouth Arts Centre, Plymouth. Touring exhibition: Cartwright Hall, Bradford; Harris Museum & Art Gallery, Preston; Herbert Gallery, Coventry; Axiom Centre for the Arts, Cheltenham; South Hill Park Arts Centre, Bracknell
1985 *Beyond Appearance*, Castle Museum, Nottingham: touring to Milton Keynes Exhibition Gallery; Wolverhampton Art Gallery; Carmarthen Museum; Oriel Theatre, Clwyd; Cooper Gallery, Barnsley
1986 *Bradford Print Biennale*, Cartwright Hall, Bradford
1987 *Premio Internazionale Biella Per L'Incisione 1987*, Turin
Black & White, Nicola Jacobs Gallery, London

1988 *Stoneworks*, Powys Castle, Welshpool, Wales
Sculpture, Waddington Galleries, London
Abstract Art from Sheffield's Collections, Mappin Art Gallery, Sheffield
1989 *The Cutting Edge*, Manchester City Art Gallery, Manchester
1992 *Sculpture*, Waddington Galleries, London
New Displays, Tate Gallery, London
Light and Shadow, Wrexham Arts Centre, Wales
Art Asia '92, New Art Centre stand, Hong Kong
1993 Sculpture Garden at Roche Court, New Art Centre, Wiltshire
1994 Tresors Fair, Singapore
1995 *British Abstract Art Part 2: Sculpture*, Flowers Gallery, London
Sculpture Garden at Roche Court, New Art Centre, Wiltshire
Journeys West, University Gallery and Firstsite at the Minories, Colchester. Touring Exhibition: Chinese Arts Centre, Manchester; Lambeth Chinese Community Association;
White Out, Curwen Gallery, London
Ka Editions, The Eagle Gallery, London
1996 *British Abstract Art Part 3: Works on Paper*, Flowers Gallery, London
1997 *Half the Sky: Chinese Women in London*, Museum of London
2015 *Art Paris*, Art Plural Gallery, Paris
2017 *Sculpture in the Close*, Jesus College, University of Cambridge
2018 *Kaleidoscope: Colour and Sequence in 1960s British Art*, Arts Council Collection Touring Exhibition: Yorkshire Sculpture Park, Wakefield; Nottingham Lakeside Arts, Nottingham; Mead Gallery, University of Warwick; Walker Art Gallery, Liverpool
Speech Acts: Reflection – Imagination – Repetition, Manchester Art Gallery, Manchester
Minimalism: Space. Light. Object. National Gallery Singapore, Singapore
Structures of Meaning | Architectures of Perception, Abu Dhabi Art Fair, Manarat Al Saadiyat, Abu Dhabi
2019 *Objects of Wonder: British Sculpture from the Tate Collection 1950s–Present*, Palais Populaire, Berlin
Suddenly Turning Visible: Art and Architecture in Southeast Asia (1969–1989), National Gallery Singapore, Singapore
2021 *Breaking the Mould: Sculpture by Women since 1945*, Arts Council Collection. Touring Exhibition: Yorkshire Sculpture Park, Wakefield; Djanogly Gallery, University of Nottingham; The Levinsky Gallery, University of Plymouth; Ferens Art Gallery, Hull; The New Art Gallery, Walsall
Hockney to Himid: 60 Years of Printmaking, Pallant House Gallery
O Canto Do Bode, Casa da Cultura, Comporta, Portugal
2022 *Creating Abstraction*, Pace Gallery, London
A Century of the Artist's Studio: 1920–2020, Whitechapel Gallery, London
Postwar Modern: New Art in Britain 1945–1965, Barbican Art Gallery, London
2023 *Taipei Biennial*, Taiwan
14th Gwangju Biennale, Korea
If Not Now, When? Generations of Women in Sculpture in Britain, 1960–2022, The Hepworth Wakefield, Wakefield

Bibliography

Ahmed, Sara. *Queer Phenomenology: Orientations, Objects, Others* (Durham, NC: Duke University Press, 2006)

Archer, Michael, 'Kim Lim Obituary', *Art Monthly*, no.213 (1998), p.17.

Arts Council of Great Britain, *Sculpture in a City: Anthony Caro, David Hall, Kim Lim, Ron Robertson-Swann, Bernard Schottlander, William Turnbull, Brian Wall, Derrick Woodham* (London: Arts Council of Great Britain, 1968).

Baring, Jo and Sarah Turner. *Sculpting Lives: Kim Lim*, podcast, Season 1, Episode 3 (released 7 April 2020).

Baro, Gene, 'The Work of Kim Lim', *Studio International: Journal of Modern Art*, vol.176, no.905 (November 1968).

Bowness, Alan. 'Introduction', in *Sculpture in the Open Air: An Exhibition of Contemporary British Sculpture in Battersea Park*, exhibition catalogue, May–September 1966 (London: GLC Parks Department, 1966).

Burn, Guy. 'Prints', *Arts Review* (1984), pp 250–51.

Cheng, Lena. 'Sculptress who works in wood', *Her World* (December 1960).

Chu, Bianca and Darren Leak (eds), *Kim Lim*, exhibition catalogue (London: Sotheby's, 2018).

Chu, Bianca. 'Kim Lim in Her Own Context', *Ocula* (11 November 2020), https://ocula.com/magazine/features/kim-lim/.

Clulow, Melanie. 'Carving a Niche', *Vogue* (July 1996).

Curtis, Penelope, 'Kim Lim', in *Sculpture in 20th Century Britain: A Guide to Sculptors in the Leeds Collections* (UK: Henry Moore Sculpture Trust, 1999).

Einzig, Hetty. *Kim Lim*, exhibition catalogue (London, Nicola Jacobs Gallery, 1982).

Elliot, Ann, *Sculpture at Goodwood – British Contemporary Sculpture* (Sussex: Cass Sculpture Foundation, Goodwood, 1995).

Flint, Charlotte. 'Liberated Form and Space', in *Postwar Modern: New Art in Britain 1945–65*, exhibition catalogue (London: Barbican Art Gallery, 2002).

Garlake, Margaret. 'Kim Lim at Nicola Jacobs Gallery Review', *Art Monthly*, no.61 (1982), p.13.

Gilmour, Pat. *Understanding Prints: A Contemporary Guide* (London: Waddington Galleries, 1979).

Gooding, Mel. 'Kim Lim; Prunella Clough', *Art Monthly,* no.92 (1986), p19.

Hooker, Denise. 'Kim Lim, Nicola Jacobs Gallery', *Arts Review* (1982).

Howarth, Jill. 'Monographs', *Kim Lim Graphics* (London: Tate Gallery Publishing, 1977).

Kee, Joan. 'Form in service of the global', in Alexander Dumbadze and Suzanne Hudson (eds), *Contemporary Art: 1989 to the Present* (Oxford: Wiley Blackwell, 2013).

Keen, Melanie and Liz Ward. *Recordings: A Select Bibliography of Contemporary African, Afro-Caribbean and Asian British Art* (London: Institute of International Visual Arts (iniva) and Chelsea College of Art and Design, 1996).

Kim Lim, exhibition catalogue (London: Waddington Galleries, 1990).

Kim Lim: Sculpting Light, exhibition catalogue (Singapore: STPI Gallery, 2018).

'Kim Lim', *The Tate Gallery 1974–6: Illustrated Catalogue of Acquisitions* (London: Tate Publishing, 1978).

King, Isabelle (ed.). *Kim Lim*, exhibition catalogue (London: Camden Arts Centre, 1999).

Leong, Weng Ka. 'Museum Eyeing Sculpture by S'pore-born Kim Lim', *The Straits Times*, 29 October 1994, p.23.

Levine, Caroline. *Forms: Whole, Rhythm, Hierarchy, Network* (Princeton, NJ: Princeton University Press, 2015).

Lilley, Claire (ed.). *Kim Lim: Sculpture and Works on Paper*, exhibition catalogue (West Yorkshire: Yorkshire Sculpture Park, 1995).

Lim, Kim. Completed survey from a questionnaire issued by Lorna Green in 1989. Now held in the archives of The Hepworth Wakefield.

Lim, Kim. Interview with Cathy Courtney. London, 20 October 1995, *National Life Stories: Artists' Lives* (London: British Library, 1995), C466/51, transcript.

Lim, Kim. 'Things in Space', *Look at Life* (1966), Rank Organisation (film).

Linton, Norbert. 'Out on a Lim', the *Guardian*, 30 September 1968.

Lippard, Lucy. 'Introduction', *Hayward Annual 1978*, exhibition catalogue (Arts Council, 1978).

Loh, Joleen. 'The Photographs of Kim Lim: A Visual Essay', *Art History*, vol.44, no.3 (2021).

Loh, Joleen and National Gallery Singapore. *The Artist Speaks: Kim Lim* (Singapore: National Gallery Singapore, 2022).

Loh, Joleen. 'Relocating Kim Lim: A Cosmopolitan Perspective', *Southeast of Now: Directions in Contemporary and Modern Art in Asia*, vol.2, no.2 (October 2018).

Mercer, Kobena. 'Iconography after Identity', in David A. Bailey, Ian Baucom and Sonia Boyce (eds), *Shades of Black: Assembling Black Arts in 1980s Britain* (Durham, NC: Duke University Press, 2005).
Ministry of Education, *First Report of the National Advisory Council on Art Education* (London: Her Majesty's Stationery Office, 1960).
Morphet, Richard. *The Tate Gallery Illustrated Catalogue of Acquisitions 1974–76* (London: Tate Gallery Publishing, 1976).
Nasar, Hammad. 'Resisting Resolution: Kim Lim's Playful Stillness', in Bianca Chu and Darren Leak (eds), *Kim Lim* (London: Sotheby's, 2018), pp 94–101.
Nasar, Hammad. 'Artistic Britishness? Questions of Nationality', in Jo Baring (ed.), *Revisiting Modern British Art* (London: Lund Humphries, 2022).
Nasar, Hammad. 'Notes from the Field: Navigating the Afterlife of the Other Story', in *Field Notes*, no.4 (Hong Kong: Asia Art Archive, 2015), pp 50–63.
Nasar, Hammad. 'Vectors of the New in Postwar Art in Britain', in *Postwar Modern: New Art in Britain 1945–65*, exhibition catalogue (London: Barbican Art Gallery, 2002), pp 23–7.
Nairne, Sandy. 'Carved. Modelled. Constructed: Three Aspects of British 20th Century Art' (London: Tate Gallery, 1977).
Nemser, Cindy. *Art Talk: Conversations with 12 Women Artists* (New York: Scribner, 1975).
Powell, Jennifer. 'A coherent, national "school" of sculpture? Constructing post-war New British Sculpture through exhibition practices', *Sculpture Journal*, vol.21, no.2 (2012), pp 37–50.
Rea, Naomi. 'More Than Two Decades After Her Death, the Great Singaporean-British Artist Kim Lim Is Finally Being Written Into Art History', *Artnet* (21 September 2020), https://news.artnet.com/art-world/kim-lim-tate-britain-1909500.
Reichardt, Jasia. 'Introduction', *Kim Lim*, exhibition catalogue (London: Axiom Gallery, 1966).
Richards, Arthur. 'S'pore girl now a sculptress in London', *Sunday Mail*, 3 July 1966.
Rombough, Howard. 'Breaking the Rules: Kim Lim', *HOT*, undated, pp 38–40.
Said, Edward. *Culture and Imperialism* (New York: Vintage, 1993).
Shapiro, Abi. 'Kim Lim: In Tune with Life and Nature', *Art Quarterly* (spring 2023), pp 25–31.
Shemza, Anwar Jalal. *A.J. Shemza: Paintings Drawings 1957–1963* (Durham: Gulbenkian Museum of Oriental Art and Archaeology, 1962).
Six Artists: Six Prints (unpublished essay). The Kim Lim archive.
Turner, Sarah Victoria and Jo Baring (eds), *Kim Lim: Sculpting Lives*, podcast, Season 1, Episode 3 (7 April 2020).
'What the critics said', *Art Monthly* (1 June 1977), p.8.

Author Biographies

Bianca Chu is strategic advisor and representative of the Kim Lim Estate and the Turnbull Studio. She is a writer, researcher, art practitioner and anthropologist based between London and Lisbon. Bianca holds a Master's Degree in History of Art & Chinese Studies from the University of Edinburgh and a Master's Degree in Material and Visual Culture in the Department of Anthropology, UCL. She is a 300HR teacher-trained Jivamukti Yoga practitioner, serves as Co-Chair of Tate Young Patrons (2020–23) and is on the advisory board of non-profit organisations Procreate Project, UK, and POR.TA Association, Portugal.

Joleen Loh is Curator at National Gallery Singapore, where her research focuses on post-war and contemporary art from Singapore and Southeast Asia. Her past exhibitions include *Nothing is Forever: Rethinking Sculpture in Singapore* and *Suddenly Turning Visible: Art and Architecture in Southeast Asia (1969–89)*. She edited the latest publication on Kim Lim for *The Artist Speaks* series (2022) and is currently working on a forthcoming exhibition of the artist at the Gallery.

Hammad Nasar is a curator, writer and strategic advisor. He is presently Senior Research Fellow at the Paul Mellon Centre (part of Yale University). His recent curatorial projects have included *Divided Selves: Legacies, Memories, Belonging* (2023), *British Art Show 9* (2021–22), *Turner Prize* (2021) and *Speech Acts: Reflection – Imagination – Repetition* (2018–19). He was awarded an MBE for services to the arts in 2023.

Dr **Abi Shapiro** is Curator at The Hepworth Wakefield with a specialist research interest in post-war sculpture and its critical histories. She has worked on curatorial projects such as *Hannah Starkey: In Real Life*, *The Art of the Potter: Sculpture and Ceramics from 1930 to Today* and *Sheila Hicks: Off Grid*. She has published research on post-war art in the *British Art Journal* and has a forthcoming book chapter with Manchester University Press about the artist Ree Morton.

Dr **Adele Tan** is Senior Curator at National Gallery Singapore. Her research focuses on modern and contemporary art in Southeast Asia and China. She also lectures in Art History at the National University of Singapore. She recently curated the 2023 Ng Teng Fong Roof Garden Commission by Mumbai-based artist Shilpa Gupta and is working on a forthcoming retrospective exhibition on Kim Lim with Joleen Loh in 2024.

Dr **Wenny Teo** is Senior Lecturer in Modern and Contemporary Art at The Courtauld Institute of Art, University of London. Her research centres on China and Sinophone cultures in transnational contexts. She is currently preparing a book on the work of Kim Lim, Li Yuan-chia and Richard Show Yu Lin, focusing on the phenomenological dimensions of space and time in their multivalent practice, as well as their entanglement with the fraught dynamics of race, migration and class in Britain from the 1960s to the 1990s.

Ming Tiampo is Professor of Art History and Co-Director of the Centre for Transnational Cultural Analysis at Carleton University. Tiampo's major projects include *Gutai: Decentering Modernism* (University of Chicago Press, 2011), *Gutai: Splendid Playground*, co-curated at the Guggenheim Museum in New York (2013), and *Jin-me Yoon* (Art Canada Institute, Toronto, 2022). Her current book *Transversal Modernism/s: The Slade School of Fine Art*, reimagines transcultural intersections through global microhistory. Tiampo is Co-Principal Investigator of Worlding Public Cultures.

Index Page numbers in **bold** refer to illustrations.

First published in 2023 by Lund Humphries in association with The Hepworth Wakefield

Published on the occasion of the exhibition
Kim Lim: Space, Rhythm & Light
The Hepworth Wakefield
25 November 2023 – 2 June 2024

Lund Humphries
Huckletree Shoreditch
Alphabeta Building
18 Finsbury Square
London EC2A 1AH
UK
www.lundhumphries.com

ISBN: 978-1-84822-666-1

A Cataloguing-in-Publication record for this book is available from the British Library

Copy edited by Michela Parkin
Designed by Joe Hales studio
Set in LL Unica77 and Gothic720 BT
Printed in Estonia

Front cover image: Kim Lim working on **Twice** (1966) in 1968
The Estate of Kim Lim. © The Lewinski Archive at Chatsworth. All Rights Reserved 2023 / Bridgeman Images
Back cover image: **Twice** (1966)

This book is printed on sustainably sourced FSC paper

The Kim Lim Estate would like to thank Andrew Cummings for his assistance with the archive of the artist.

Image credits
All photos unless otherwise stated are © Estate of Kim Lim. All Rights Reserved, DACS 2023

Courtesy The Hepworth Wakefield: 1 and 48 (photographer: Nick Singleton)
Courtesy Arts Council Collection, Southbank Centre, London. © Estate of Kim Lim. All rights reserved, DACS, 2011: 16, 65
Andrew Catlin: 80
Courtesy The Estate of Kim Lim: 2, 3, 4 (photographer Grace Lau), 5, 6, 7 (photographer Sotheby's Collection: collection of Chong Huai Seng and Ning Chong, Singapore), 8, 9 (photographer Mark Dalton), 10, 11, 12, 13, 14, 15, 17, 18, 19, 20, 21, 22, 23, 24, 25, 26, 27, 28, 29, 30 (photographer George Meyrick), 31, 32 (photographer Grace Lau), 33, 34, 35, 36, 37, 38, 39, 40, 41, 42, 43, 44, 45, 46, 47 (photographer Kenneth Koh), 49, 50, 52, 53, 54, 55, 56, 57 (photographer Kim Lim), 58 (photographer Mark Dalton), 59, 60, 61, 62, 63, 64, 66, 67, 69, 70, 71 (photographer Kim Lim), 74, 75, 76, 77, 78, 79, 82, 83, 84, 85 (photographer Kim Lim), 86
Kenneth Griffiths: 51
© The Lewinski Archive at Chatsworth. All Rights Reserved 2023 / Bridgeman Images: cover, 87
Courtesy Lim Chong Keat and Singapore National Gallery: 81
Courtesy of National Heritage Board, Singapore: 68, 70, 72, 73